FOUCAULT AT THE MOVIES

FOUCAULT
AT THE MOVIES

Michel Foucault
Patrice Maniglier
Dork Zabunyan

Translated and edited by Clare O'Farrell

Columbia University Press   *New York*

COLUMBIA
UNIVERSITY
PRESS

Columbia University Press gratefully acknowledges
the generous support for this book provided by
Publisher's Circle member Bruno A. Quinson.

Columbia University Press
Publishers Since 1893
New York   Chichester, West Sussex
cup.columbia.edu

This work, published as part of a program of aid for publication,
received support from the Institut Français.

Excerpts from DITS ET ECRITS (1954–1988) by Michel Foucault, under
the direction of Daniel Defert and François Ewald with the collaboration
of Jacques Lagrange, copyright © 1994 Editions Gallimard, Paris
Foucault va au Cinema copyright © 2011 Bayard Editions

Library of Congress Cataloging-in-Publication Data
Names: Maniglier, Patrice, author. | Zabunyan, Dork, author.
Title: Foucault at the movies / Michel Foucault, Patrice Maniglier,
Dork Zabunyan; translated and edited by Clare O'Farrell.
Other titles: Foucault va au cinéma. English
Description: New York: Columbia University Press, 2018. |
Includes bibliographical references and index.
Identifiers: LCCN 2018007537 | ISBN 9780231167079 (pbk.) |
ISBN 9780231167062 (cloth)
Subjects: LCSH: Foucault, Michel, 1926–1984. |
Motion pictures—Philosophy.
Classification: LCC B2430.F724 M3513 2018 | DDC 791.43—dc23
LC record available at https://lccn.loc.gov/2018007537

Cover image: Michel Foucault and Maurice Clavel at a demonstration
against the murder of Pierre Overney, 28 Febuary 1972 (detail) /
Private Collection / Photo copyright © AGIP / Bridgeman Images

CONTENTS

TRANSLATOR'S PREFACE

This is a larger book than the original French publication. The complete versions (rather than extracts) of Foucault's interviews, reviews, and articles on film are all presented here. These are translations of the versions published in the collection of Foucault's shorter writings in French, *Dits et écrits*.[1] I have added extra references to help clarify sources and points of detail for an English-language audience, and existing English translations of work originally referred to in French have been cited. All films are referred to by their official English title where these exist. The short appendix lists the films shown at a series of special events organized in 2011 by Dork Zabunyan and Patrice Maniglier around Foucault and film.

In a number of cases, I have given different titles to Foucault's pieces to make them more descriptive or work better in English. The original French titles were not Foucault's but those of newspaper, magazine, and journal editors, and they either don't translate well into English or are somewhat nondescript (for example, "interview"). The chapters by Foucault are in chronological order of original publication, and details about their original publication are provided at the head of the notes section for each chapter.

I owe a considerable debt to Jennifer Crewe at Columbia University Press for her patience and support from the start to the finish of this project. Patrice Maniglier and Dork Zabunyan provided valuable comments and suggestions on the translation of their chapters. Stuart Elden, Colin Gordon, and Daniele Lorenzini have been wonderful companions in the enjoyable task of the dissemination of Foucault's work and I acknowledge them here. I would also like to thank Chris Rojek for his encouragement and help over many years. Suzanne Carrington at Queensland University of Technology provided appreciated support. I am grateful to Naomi Stekelenburg in particular and to Megan Kimber for formatting the manuscript to very tight deadlines and also to Judy Gregory for helpful comments in relation to aspects of style in the Foucault translations. Many other people, friends and family, have contributed to this project in various and essential ways and I would like to thank them all.

INTRODUCTION

Michel Foucault's Cut

PATRICE MANIGLIER AND DORK ZABUNYAN

The relationship between film and history has been the subject of much discussion over the last few years. Strangely, Michel Foucault's name is virtually absent from this debate. Although, strictly speaking, we don't find any sustained treatment of film in Foucault's work, there is a general awareness that he did occasionally cross paths with film, even if his bibliography is somewhat limited on this score. There was even a festival organized by the Cinémathèque Française in 2004 around this encounter titled "Foucault—Cinema—Image Memory, Image, Power."[1] Yet it doesn't seem to have occurred to anyone to deal with this encounter in any systematic way. This book aims to fill this gap.

Foucault's first excursion into film was from a historical standpoint, and the first text where he deals explicitly with film is proof of this. This text, titled "Film, History, and Popular Memory," was published in 1974 in the form of an interview conducted by the editors of *Cahiers du cinéma*. They asked Foucault about certain forms involving the emergence and persistence of the past and a very particular past at that, namely, the Second World War and the twin themes of the French Occupation and the Resistance. Foucault resituates these themes in a distinction, which we will return to later, between the epic and narrative forms of official historiography and those forms that he terms the "popular memory of struggles," which are persistently stifled and have to be continually revived.

Foucault's encounter with the moving image draws its essence from this historical terrain, a terrain that is inextricably linked to the present. This encounter is so profound and so real that it fulfills all our expectations of what we might hope for in a dialogue between philosophical activity and artistic practice. In this case, philosophy is not content to simply treat art as an object but is able to pursue its own concerns through art in such a way that both art and philosophy are able to reinvent themselves via various short cuts and montages, both then setting out again on paths that neither had dreamed of following. Thus the critics at the *Cahiers* and then a director (René Allio) take up the problem Foucault raised in 1973 with the publication of Pierre Rivière's memoir.[2] In this case someone speaks, "even if he has no voice,"[3] breaking with all the dogmatisms of discourse. For his part, Foucault discovers in the films of Marguerite Duras and Werner Schroeter a new way of "disorganizing" bodies, a prelude to a new use of pleasures.[4]

All this leads us to comment on the nature of the dialogue between philosophy and film that motivates *Foucault at the Movies*. It is a fact: "film-philosophy" is in fashion. There are countless publications in both French and English that claim to reflect on film or philosophize using the image. Yet this enthusiasm is overwhelmingly dominated by an approach that consists in finding illustrations of philosophical arguments in film. Plato's cave can be found in the Wachowskis' film *The Matrix*, and Lacan's psychoanalysis in Hitchcock's anxieties. While this game certainly has the merit of being entertaining and educational, it's not clear that it provides anything really new. Aspects

that are specific to film are neglected at the expens[
and readers of Plato know from the outset that th[
nothing further by shutting themselves up in a dar[
ater. Can we do better than this? Perhaps we can.

We might remember that we can ask philosophers not just
to tell us what to think but, more important, to set out what the
requirements of thought in action are, without this thought necessarily needing to take us in one direction or another. In the
same way, film doesn't merely represent events, it teaches us to
"see otherwise" without necessarily constraining us to see in a
particular way. As a consequence, we can set up operations rather
than content face-to-face, with concepts on one side and images
on the other. We can compare philosophical and cinematic works,
not as two ways of saying the same thing in distinct media but
as two approaches that deal with the same problem in accordance
with their respective modes of expression. Philosophy can discover more and better things in film than the illustration of
truths to which concepts already provide access. To emphasize
here, philosophers can find in film a partner, a rival, an inspiration, a place where an experiment can be conducted in what it
means to think otherwise.

"Thinking otherwise": the phrase is Foucault's; one can certainly find films in the history of cinema that illustrate Foucault's
arguments on madness, disciplinary societies, and prisons. Such
films do indeed exist. But we might also note that Foucault was
primarily seeking another way of doing history, a history that
was committed to bringing *events* to the fore without submit-
ting them to the linearity of narrative. It was essentially a matter
of pointing out what was happening at the "edge" of our present, a present of which we might be the contemporaries without
necessarily being the heroes. But hasn't one of the promises of
film been to single out events without telling a story and without

XII % PATRICE MANIGLIER AND DORK ZABUNYAN

locking them into a narrative thread in which we find value-driven heroes transforming the situation through reconciliatory action? Hasn't cinema promised to show an entire and sometimes barely perceptible world of nonhuman actions? Foucault himself saw that film opened up the possibility of grasping this "molecular" history that pays scant regard to either the freedom of humans as masters of their destiny or the efficacy of grand unconscious structures. The focus of this history is instead on those "micro procedures" of which we are unaware but which nonetheless decide on some of the most profound changes affecting our relation to ourselves and the world. Further, it is a history that captures that "dust of the battle" that Foucault sought to reconstruct behind the grand periodicities of changes of regime and laws. It is a nonheroic history that in many ways echoes the very nature of those "events" that constituted May '68.

The questions that run through *Foucault at the Movies* could therefore be formulated as follows: In what sense does film allow history to be done otherwise? Does film allow those tiny elements that make up the cogs of what Foucault describes as a "technology of power" to be assessed and displayed in all their unexpected and rigorous arrangements? Can film contribute to a critique of our present, exposing principles that other modes of representation simply miss? In other words, we will be considering what contribution film is able to make to all those today who are interested in taking up the archaeological approach proposed by Foucault in one way or another. At the same time, we shall also examine the problems this approach raises in relation to the cinematic image and its components, evolution, and mutations. In part 1 of this volume, our starting point is, and remains, the ten texts in part 2 that the philosopher dedicated to film's moving images. Foucault's major works will naturally be referred to in the course of the analysis—from *The Archaeology of Knowledge*

to *The Use of Pleasures*, from "The Order of Discou
pline and Punish—but our aim is not simply to lir
to establishing parallels between different aspects (
work of which the spoken and written words on film ⌐... a part.
In other words, we want to leave the comfort of exegesis behind
and situate ourselves at the level of the *effects* produced by these
interviews, "conversations," and other articles by Foucault on
film.

Four effects emerge broadly in the pages that follow: the
first is the effect on film criticism, which makes practical use of
Foucault's thought. This is with a view to understanding the
modifications that affect what Foucault himself has to say about
particular films and the history of cinema. Next, there is the
effect on the theory and aesthetics of film. Even if Foucault
doesn't explore questions of paradigm or essence, the idea of the
specificity of film as an art form is certainly emphasized
throughout the interviews in terms of moving images being
linked to relations of power, conduct in relation to love, or, further, the story of a struggle. We have already mentioned the
effect on the practice of philosophy. In this instance, the texts on
film will be used to extract, that is, to construct, a concept of the
event that will in turn illuminate a corresponding metaphysics
in Foucault's work. Equally, there is the effect on historical
inquiry that emerges over the course of several interviews. The
archivist was strongly invested in a close connection between
film and knowledge, a connection that Foucault was very much
committed to, even going so far as to claim that film might be
able to "reappraise" knowledge.[5]

A fifth effect might be envisaged, which we cannot anticipate
of course, namely, the potential effect produced by Foucault's
own writings and ideas on directors themselves. We are not
talking here about period adaptations relating to eras dealt with

in his books (for example, the classical age or the disciplinary society) or of faithful reconstructions of library archives (a film on nineteenth-century "infamous men" perhaps?), or an imagined portrait of Foucault the philosopher. Instead, perhaps we could envisage a film that takes up on its own terms in some other situation the questions Foucault raised, questions that the present work operating at the crossroads of philosophy, history, and film would like to bring into the spotlight.[6]

FOUCAULT AT THE MOVIES

PART I

FOUCAULT AND FILM

A Historical and Philosophical Encounter

1

WHAT FILM IS ABLE TO DO

Foucault and Cinematic Knowledge

DORK ZABUNYAN

n the entry on Foucault from the "Dictionary" at the end of
the June 1981 issue of *Cahiers du cinéma*, Serge Daney declared
that Michel Foucault was, for the *Cahiers*, "a constant, irreplaceable, and essential reference."[1] What are we to make of this
reverence of film enthusiasts for a philosopher who once declared
he knew nothing about "the aesthetics" of film?[2] This somewhat
mischievous confession actually disguises a real connection
with moving images, a connection that commentators have
neglected. In spite of this, it's possible to advance at least three
reasons explaining the critics' enthusiasm for the author of
The Order of Things, both during his lifetime and beyond.[3] First,
we need to consider the way Foucault's work directly or indirectly
inspired several critics and directors in the wake of *Cahiers du
cinéma*. Jacques Rivette, who was editor-in-chief of the *Cahiers*
from 1963 to 1965, read *Raymond Roussel* with enthusiasm when
it was published in 1963.[4] In the late 1960s other writers at the
journal hastened to Vincennes to attend Foucault's course. Still
others, like Jean Narboni, came up with new angles on the notion
of the *auteur* using the philosopher's texts on "writing without a
subject" in the work of Beckett, Kafka, and Mallarmé.[5] This
was an important contribution that allows a retrospective

understanding of the formal and critical scope of the *politique des auteurs* initiated by *Cahiers du cinéma*. This was also taken up by the journal at the same time in parallel with what was happening in the *Nouveau Roman* in literature. It's not the actual figure of the author who is "dead," the author who signs the work, organizes its elements, and gives it a style; rather, it's the "author-function" that conflates the practice of art with the first-person subject. This conflation excludes creative functions where the conquest of the impersonal is inseparable from an intensification of experience.

A second event, because it was indeed an event, offers the first hint of a union between Foucault and the film world. The world of film criticism: *Cahiers du cinéma*—them again—sought Foucault out in person asking him to contribute to discussions on the art of moving images. This occurred in the form of an interview appearing in the summer issue for 1974.[6] This interview took place at a particular moment in the history of the journal, which at the time was trying to distance itself from the "Maoist years" it had just gone through. This position was both too dogmatic as well as too comfortable for the interviewers, Pascal Bonitzer, Serge Toubiana, and Serge Daney.[7] This was because the *Cahiers* at the time was making pronouncements on current events without the necessary modesty that might have allowed for a more complex grasp of the situation. Calling on Foucault in a political context dominated by the dispiriting election of Valéry Giscard d'Estaing to the presidency could equally well be understood as the wish to establish some distance from a rigid critical position in relation to current affairs. It could also correspondingly be understood as a desire to occupy a position that renewed a grasp on reality, without reinstating a position that failed to come to terms both with the struggles of a turbulent period and with the unpredictable representation of those struggles in film. For Toubiana, "Foucault's essential contribution in this interview in *Cahiers du cinéma* is the critique of a restrictive and mechanistic Marxist vision of power tied strictly to economics."[8] In addition, Bonitzer, Toubiana, and Daney were strongly opposed to the "fashion for retro" that was fossilizing a still vibrant past on screens—that of the Second World War with all its compromises and its collaborations. So they wanted to meet with Foucault to record his views on two films that had been released almost simultaneously, namely, Louis Malle's *Lacombe, Lucien* (1974) and Liliana Cavani's *The Night Porter* (1973). Both were symbols of the "fashion for retro," which prevented the darkest pages of history from throwing light onto the present. It was a fashion that at the same time silenced the voices of those who, even in defeat, had known how to escape the snares of an omniscient power, even if only for a moment.

PIERRE RIVIÈRE'S MEMOIR: A "CROSS-CHECK" FOR CINEPHILES

A double imperative led the *Cahiers* to make contact with Foucault. One was the rejection of an overarching position on the present and its myriad struggles, and the other was the rejection of a "fashion" that obliterated historical vagaries, discontinuities, and departures from the norm. This double imperative found its partial origin in a work presented by the philosopher in 1973, when he was examining the links between psychiatry and penal justice at the College of France. This was *I, Pierre Rivière, Having Slaughtered My Mother, My Sister and My Brother . . .* , a memoir "written by the accused himself, a peasant of some twenty years of age who claimed that he could 'only barely read and write,' and who had undertaken during his detention on remand to give 'particulars and an explanation' of his crime."[9] What struck the editors of the *Cahiers* about this book was the analytical power of a writing that, although not rooted in any preestablished knowledge, was still the repository of relations of power (legal, police, medical, and so on) and in spite of itself managed to confound established knowledge. It was a voice that subscribed to no doctrine, creating a vacuum around itself through this nonadherence. At the same time, the memoir proclaimed the beginnings of a voice beyond the crime to which it bore witness, a voice that could not be reclaimed, a voice, as Foucault writes, that frustrates "the whole range of tactics by which we can try to reconstitute it, situate it, and give it its status as the discourse of either a madman or a criminal."[10]

In the *Cahiers* issue that followed the 1974 interview, Serge Daney restated the conditions that allowed for the existence of a truly "anti-retro" cinema and signaled the importance of the editorial project on Rivière precisely in terms of its potential effects on "leftist" film production. Louis Malle's film is used as a starting point for discussion: "Is there something that exists, *in film* (in this specific arrangement of images and sounds), that could be opposed to *Lacombe, Lucien* today? No. But in another quite heterogeneous field (history? literature?), Foucault's work on Pierre Rivière provides the possibility of performing a cross-check against the Mallean theme of the 'primitive, pawn of a blind history.'"[11] It's a "cross-check" that goes hand in hand with the creation of popular memory (we'll come back to this later), and which also raises another problem of how to establish a form of fiction which doesn't eliminate the past, regardless of what social category is invoked in all its presumed alienation. Daney pursues his investigation in these terms, with continuing reference to Rivière: "How can we consider Lacombe as anything other than a barbarian (lacking in humanity) or retarded (lacking in knowledge and education)? When Foucault speaks of Rivière, what he emphasizes is that Rivière writes that if he is deficient in knowledge, he is not deficient in discourse *or memory*. Alienated doesn't mean ahistorical."[12]

It's in this sense that the reading of Pierre Rivière contributes indirectly to an escape from a profoundly amnesiac tradition characterized in film by the "fashion for retro." The editors of the *Cahiers* say as much when they claim, in conversation with Foucault, that if "Pierre Rivière is a man who writes, who executes a murder and who has a quite extraordinary memory, Malle, on the other hand, treats his hero as a half-wit, as someone who goes through everything—history, war, collaboration— without gaining anything from his experience."[13] This is a fruitful comparison, despite the obvious dissimilarity in trajectories, and one that throws light on the apparent paradox of the Rivière case. Here, memory unfolds in all its meanders and layers, while running the risk of surrounding itself with silence, but this silence is less the effect of the calm deployment of memory than the result of an unimaginable act: a person "speaks even if he has no voice," as the *Cahiers* notes again soberly.[14] We can see here the inklings of a discourse that has no point of reference, one that is light years away from the oppressive period during which the magazine uttered a few rigid and intimidating judgments. *I, Pierre Rivière* in fact acted as a "cross-check" on two fronts: against a practice of film criticism that had become too rigid and orthodox, and also against a way of filming that "memorized nothing" (Daney) and shied away from the transformations of history (from past to present and vice versa).[15]

"Film, History, and Popular Memory" starts with a topical issue relating to the "political situation" that was one of the ingredients contributing to the fashion for retro. The election of Giscard, which was linked to the obsolescence, indeed the death, of Gaullism, was not without its effects on understandings of the Resistance in France. Foucault relates this theme to contemporary struggles, associating it with the elaboration of the memory of popular struggles. A notion that is integral to this context, "the eroticization of power,"[16] also runs through the philosopher's other interviews on film. Foucault describes this problem as "serious," and it runs through these interviews, either implicitly, as in "The Nondisciplinary Camera Versus Sade,"[17] where Foucault criticizes Pier Paolo Pasolini's *Salò* (1975), or just beneath the surface, as in "The Four Horsemen of the Apocalypse,"[18] where he engages in a discussion with Bernard Sobel on Hans-Jürgen Syberberg's film *Hitler: A Film from Germany* (1977). This problem "that won't go away" is "how do we love power?" How do we understand this "desire for power" that makes us love what alienates us but gives us pleasure at the same time?[19] As Serge Daney suggested in the early 1980s, this is where we can see the third factor that accounts for the "constant" and "essential" presence of Michel Foucault in certain areas of film criticism and theory. It's not a simple matter here of tracking Foucault's influence on film by locating it within the general intellectual ferment of the 1960s and 1970s. Neither is it a matter of locating the origins of that inspiration in the "Film, History, and Popular Memory" interview in the *Cahiers*. Instead, it's a matter of reflecting on the intersections between film and the philosopher's work, taking into account ideas from the other works that make up his writings and ideas that appear in his interviews and remarks on film. Ultimately, one of the aims of the current analysis is to determine where film fits into the system of knowledge described by Foucault, and how film undertakes a "reappraisal" of this system from the standpoint of the "great divide between knowledge and art," which is "in the process of breaking down."[20]

A FILM-EFFECT

What connections and short circuits exist between film and Foucault's books? Was Foucault's work able to find a way of extending thought through film, leading to a genuine film-effect? Could the experience of film have produced a shift in his philosophical work, possibly heralding a fragment of the work that was to come? The theme of the eroticization of power has just been mentioned, and its appearance in the 1974 interview can certainly be situated within the perspective of the work done for *The History of Sexuality*, the first volume of which appeared in 1976. This "history of sexuality" in addition claimed to be "a series of studies concerning the historical relationships of power and the discourse on sex."[21] These studies would lead Foucault to simultaneously write an article in 1977 on *Love Meetings* (1964), "the enquiry into sexuality" directed by Pasolini in the early 1960s, where "the ecosystem of sex" is assessed in relation to the economic development of Italy as well as the transformation of family practices and the legal changes that followed from this.[22] The other volumes of *The History of Sexuality* are also anticipated by a "conversation" that precedes their publication. In an apparently informal exchange with Werner Schroeter in December 1981,[23] Foucault returns to *The Death of Maria Malibran* (1972), which he had already reviewed in 1975 for *Cinématographe*,[24] and cites *Willow Springs* (1973) by the same director. We also see in this discussion the formulation of a way of thinking that resonates with the work on the Greeks that Foucault was undertaking for *The Use of Pleasure* and *The*

Care of the Self (both published in 1984).[25] Having distinguished "love" from "passion"—love being a mutually agreed on experience of appropriation and ownership, whereas passion entails "mobile" affects and "unnamed" relationships—Foucault admits to an increasing interest in the manifestations of an "art of living," right down to the most everyday experience: "I make no distinction between those who make their lives a work of art and those who create artistic work during their lives. A life can be a perfect and sublime work: this was something the Greeks knew, but which we have completely forgotten, especially since the Renaissance."[26]

The reflexive lines between film and Foucault's writings can of course be found elsewhere in his work before the publication of the volumes on *The History of Sexuality*. We have drawn attention to the way in which the publication of Pierre Rivière's memoir led to the *Cahiers du cinema*'s desire to meet the philosopher. It was probably another book that led the magazine to organize an interview with René Féret in January 1976.[27] Féret was the director of *The Story of Paul* (1975), a film about the asylum and the relations of power between patients and doctors. Féret's filming was virtually contemporary with *Discipline and Punish*,[28] and it's not by chance that the interview deals with the "specific effect" produced by "the space of the asylum, its walls, its system of coexistence and hierarchy" and by the experience of filming itself. Neither is it by chance that Foucault emphasizes again "a whole series of mechanisms and effects that are specific to the institution of the asylum" that exist in such a way that we are saying "it was not *like* the asylum" but rather "it *was* the asylum."[29] Foucault also draws attention to the way film shows how medical power contributes to the disciplinary society, "taking over" from writing while at the same time producing a different effect, "not at the level of what we know" but at the level of our ways of acting, doing, and thinking.[30] Foucault is commenting on René Allio's *I, Pierre Rivière* (1976), but this remark applies equally well to Féret's film.[31] A paradox emerges on this front that is worth analyzing. If the separation between knowledge and art (which includes film) is becoming increasingly less evident according to Foucault, the growing connection between these two domains doesn't necessarily lead film into the field occupied by knowledge. In other words, if film "reappraises" what knowledge is and doesn't seem to be a form of knowledge itself, this doesn't mean that knowledge is "disqualified." Of course, film is situated beyond the discursive, but it can't be identified with the nondiscursive, which corresponds to the other side of knowledge in Foucault's work. Even if statements and visibilities do indeed constitute the two poles of knowledge, the art of moving images is not captured within this framework of knowledge and the visible in the texts that the philosopher devotes to film. This is different from his treatment of the Velázquez painting at the beginning of *The Order of Things*,[32] or Magritte in "This Is Not a Pipe,"[33] or Manet (the projected monograph on *Le noir et la couleur*).[34] We will demonstrate later how moving images (and sounds) can operate within the field of knowledge through a historical "effect" that derives from film itself, and its capacity to "convey a sense of history" while not attempting to act as a substitute for history as "a scholarly activity" that is "academic and takes place in universities."[35]

Foucault takes for granted the combination of the words "cinema" and "knowledge," even if it is something that hasn't happened yet. If the order of visibilities is located at the level of what we know and in various points of friction with established powers,[36] this order is arranged in accordance with an experience of the body that is not necessarily associated with knowledge. An example of this might be the conversation with

Hélène Cixous on Marguerite Duras,[37] which also deals with the cinematic work of the author of *Moderato cantabile*.[38] In this discussion, Foucault reflects on how Duras's written and visual work are able to exist together. The books are defined by "gestures" or "gazes" that are caught up in a constant process of decomposition. On the other hand, the films display a multitude of "sudden emergences," here a simple "gesture," there an "eye." But this distinction between texts that tend to "annul" beings and a cinema of sudden emergences where characters seem "[to come] out of the fog" doesn't form a division in itself, let alone a definitive opposition. The proof lies in the actor Michael Lonsdale, the vice-consul *of India Song* (1975), who in himself embodies these two tendencies on the screen. In fact, "we don't know what his form is. We don't know what his face is like. Does Lonsdale have a nose, does Lonsdale have a chin? Does he have a smile? I really don't know. He is thick and solid like a formless fog," a diffuse silhouette, without defined contours, on the verge of disappearance. But this same body generates "rumblings from who knows where, rumblings which are his voice, or again his gestures which are not attached to anything," a series of striking emergences that nonetheless depend on no identifiable presence. This leads Foucault to the following conclusion: "It seems to me that Lonsdale is absolutely one with Duras's text, or rather with this mixture of text/image."[39]

When connected to film, literature seems to become detached from the spheres of knowledge with which it is most often associated. For example, we might consider the way literary references function in the *History of Madness*,[40] where the names of writers reveal the other or the boundaries of an era as well as facilitating the interpretation of that era from within.[41] The discussion with Hélène Cixous doesn't allow for the clarification of the status of Marguerite Duras's texts within the historical situation that gave birth to them; but this is probably not the purpose of this friendly conversation, which doesn't call on the archivist's practice in this context. What remains is this displacement of writing to the surface of the actor's body, which potentially gives us a clue as to the place film occupies in Foucault's reflection. In any case, it's not a matter of coming to grips with the writing here as it is transposed, or even transformed, into film dialogue, since the sound component is not examined on its own terms. It's a matter of emphasizing how the performer's body becomes the place where two tendencies coexist in Marguerite Duras's work, namely, in the dissolution and the emergence of forms that are always imprecise. This "mixture of text/image" involves a corporeal experience that is not unrelated to "this constantly mobile state," the "unstable moment" that is "passion" and which achieves "unnameable qualities" as Foucault states in 1982 in "Werner Schroeter and Michel Foucault in Conversation." In 1975 Foucault had already noted in relation to Schroeter's *The Death of Maria Malibran* a "reduction, a granulation of the body, a kind of autonomous exaltation of its smallest parts, of the minutest potentials of a fragment of the body."[42] This breaking down of the "organicity" of the body (Schroeter) or the highlighting of the evanescent character of its features or functions (Duras) asserts itself as an essential aspect of Foucault's interest in film.

If work on the archive doesn't grant film as prominent a place in the archaeology of knowledges as novels or painting, and if moving images only touch on the articulation of archaeology with the effects of power without developing this in any depth, the motif of the body, to some extent, confirms the hypothesis advanced above. The exposition of this motif in the texts on film heralds a development that is expressed after the publication of the first volume of *The History of Sexuality*, a work almost without an exterior, where the different "mechanisms" of sexuality remain fundamentally intertwined with strategies of power. The vast enterprise of *The History of Sexuality* favors the body and pleasures in "counter[ing] the grips of power" that seek "to subject us to that austere monarchy of sex,"[43] and the remarks on certain films can be seen to be part of this work, even if these remarks do not directly invoke these various "grips."[44] These remarks signal an effective exit through images and sound from the constraining apparatuses (*dispositifs*) of sexuality—regardless of the "liberation" they might promise us. This is evidenced in the call for a "nondisciplinary eroticism" in the first text on Schroeter in 1975, where Foucault invokes a "body in a volatile and diffuse state, with its chance encounters and uncalculated pleasures."[45] These lines are not without resonance with the 1977 pages on Pasolini's *Love Meetings*, that is, meetings or even a "forum" on love, something that is "at a far remove from the confessional" and in any case takes part, in its own way, in apparatuses of sexuality through a determination to talk about sex—even if, remarkably, there is no "ferment of sexuality" or festival of sex on the agenda here.[46] As we have already stated, a manifesto for "beyond" disciplinary eroticism is certainly expressed in the "conversation" with Schroeter. Here Foucault is demonstrably most impressed by the way in which the German filmmaker manages to avoid any psychological determination in the relationship between the characters. It's as if through films he had been able to establish one of the "counterattacks" against the apparatus of sexuality mentioned at the end of the first volume of *The History of Sexuality*, and which the following volumes undertake in a different context, after a detour through antiquity.[47] As Foucault mentions in the same conversation, "the art of living means killing psychology." Among other things, it is about allowing oneself to be enveloped by a "passion" that is both obvious and elusive, while at the same time avoiding the question of its initial appearance and what it is to become. In other words, it's a matter of achieving "at every instant" between beings "a coloration, a shape, and an intensity to something which never says what it is."[48] Of course, "we see bodies, faces, lips, and eyes," but only in the light of a mystery whose origins one searches for in vain.[49] It's a place where one can find a subterranean relationship with the text on Duras, with Lonsdale's body and "his voice, or again his gestures which are not attached to anything which come through the screen towards you." Here we find evidence of a body that resists identification, of a character who escapes any psychological hold.

FOUCAULT'S CINEMATIC ASCETICISM, OR THE SPECIFICITY OF FILM

Besides allowing the creation of links between the scattered fragments of Foucault's work, and its reconfiguration around their points of tension, the theme of the filmed body also raises a question that is difficult to avoid when one begins to examine the role moving images play in the philosopher's words and writings. This is the question of what is specific about film beyond the paradigm of the medium. Contrary to appearances, Foucault's texts offer a number of substantial indications on this front. The body, in particular, plays a role in distinguishing film from theater, suggesting the existence of something unique to film. When asked about *Some Like It Hot* (1959) and the romantic relationship between Marilyn Monroe and Tony Curtis in this film, Foucault argues that this relationship remains at a primarily theatrical level in the sense of "the actors taking the sacrifice of the hero upon themselves and realizing it within their own bodies," whereas what is new in Schroeter, for example, is "the discovery and exploration of the body using the camera."[50] What film can do much more clearly than theater is disaggregate bodies and the "unnameable" and "unusable" that is concealed within them. This is an assertion that emerges in the wake of a confrontation with Sade, for whom the body obeys a cold and precise hierarchy of organs, in contrast to the pleasures presumed to arise from exploiting or turning the way the body is used upside down. Film, in other words, is among those arts that allow the best view—in any case a better view than theater—of this "great wonder of the fragmented body."

In this same 1975 interview, Foucault presents other arguments that put us on the track of something unique to film. These arguments are not based on a comparative study with other art forms, asserting the superiority of one form or another (for example, theater as opposed to film, as was the common argument in the 1920s and 1930s). He doesn't take a modernist approach either, an approach that establishes film's potential in terms of the expressive virtualities of its technical mechanisms, an angle inspired by Clement Greenberg and his writings on American painting.[51] Rather, we can observe the way in which Foucault celebrates directors who manage to make film an "art of poverty,"[52] even if the medium of film is meant instead to embellish reality or succumb to the "supplementary play of the camera."[53] This significant statement, which appears in "The Nondisciplinary Camera Versus Sade," concerns precisely the possibility of bringing the work of Sade to the screen. Foucault is categorical: "There's nothing more allergic to film than the work of Sade." The rituals and the other regulations conceived of by the author of *Justine* are "carefully planned" and always take the "rigorous forms of ceremony." How can this set of scrupulous protocols be reconciled with an art in which every camera movement and every sequence of shots generate either an addition to or a subtraction from the representation of the real? In fact, for Sade, "the moment anything goes missing or is superimposed, all is lost." This is why film—the art of the image where the real is augmented by a mechanical eye (the camera) or diminished by the ellipses of fragmented editing—is incompatible with Sade's writings.

Foucault's words are the prelude to a critique of Liliana Cavani's *The Night Porter* and Pasolini's *Salò, or the 120 Days of Sodom* (1975), both of which, on different fronts, make a "total historical error" in elaborating a rereading of Nazism or fascism in the light of figures from the world of Sade. Nazism was not born of the dreams of "grand twentieth-century erotic madmen" but rather of "the disgusting petty-bourgeois dream of racial cleanliness that underlay the Nazi dream."[54] These words form part of a broader denunciation of an eroticism closely linked to the disciplinary society, of which sadism in some ways forms the paradigm. Our purpose is not to assess this statement concerning the lack of correspondence between Sade and the moving image. Rather, it is to seize on this lack of correspondence and produce a counteruse of this image that might upset "the supplementary play of the camera" in a positive way revealing, if not an ontology, then at least something that is unique to film in Foucault's work. A counteruse of this type exists, as we know, in Schroeter's work where the camera succeeds in showing how bodies can be fragmented, transforming the mundane exercise of their constituent organs. Here the body "becomes a landscape, a caravan, a storm, a mountain of sand, and so on."[55] The singularity of film, however, is not limited to this reasoned experience of corporeal dismantlement; it is also, and especially, woven into a certain sobriety of images: an "art of poverty," as we have said. Foucault uses the term in the discussion on Marguerite Duras and relates it, to begin with, to the literary part of her work. Here poverty is a reference to the conquest of a "memory without remembering"; "a memory of memory with each memory erasing all remembering, and so on indefinitely."[56] Foucault then wonders how what is at work in the texts can find a new expression in images and declares to this effect that this memory without remembering is like "a kind of fog," a phrase that precisely defines the characters' bodies on the screen (Lonsdale as "a formless fog"). In other words, the art of poverty with which Duras experiments in her writings finds its extension in film in this "sudden emergence" of corporeal fragments—"a gesture, a gaze"—that underpin a kind of asceticism of the camera whose images literally pierce the screen. It is in this sense that Foucault describes Lonsdale's body, drawing attention to Duras's construction of a "third dimension, where only the third dimension is left without the other two to support it so that it's always in front of you, it's always between the screen and you, it's never either on or in the screen." Duras's cinematographic ascesis, which completely modifies "the supplementary play of the camera," consists in this: the images of bodies become detached from their medium (the screen) and enter into a gaseous state that is in sharp contrast to the simple impression of presence (on the screen). In a way, this is where the proof lies—without this, we cannot speak of asceticism in the sense Foucault uses it in *The Use of Pleasure*—or the shattering of all representation, which the "third dimension" of *India Song* or *Destroy, She Said* (1969) leads to.

Sobriety and asceticism in moving images is the main characteristic of film, the "specific" requirement that Foucault assigns to it, regardless of the "granulation" of bodies or the transcending of systems of representation that it favors. What is remarkable is that this characteristic can be found in the philosopher's other texts on other directors. For example, when Foucault praises René Féret for his capacity for making the actual effects of internment visible in *The Story of Paul*, at the same time he pays homage to the way in which "each gesture is stripped down to its maximum intensity" in the patients and physicians. It's as if "this stripping down" is the necessary condition for creating a vision of the way the institution of the asylum works on film.[57] Foucault continues to apply this idea in explaining how René Allio manages to avoid the pitfall of a historical reconstruction of Pierre Rivière's crime. A reconstruction, being too preoccupied with an artificial resemblance to the past, would fix the event in such a way that it would no longer work on our present. Foucault evokes the prowess of Allio's direction in these terms: "It's a difficult feat to reduce the entire cinematic apparatus, the whole apparatus of film to such economy, and that is truly extraordinary, quite unique, I think, in the history of film."[58] Here again the reduction of the "cinematic apparatus" is accompanied by a use of the camera that opposes its "supplementary action" and all that relates to the false or illusory, as Bresson would have said, or which applies a "museum-like ointment" over things and actions, as Daney would have it.[59] In fact, the risk is that film can turn the past into a decorative entity, where the archive becomes a collector's item, hampering the capture of historical discontinuities. Allio circumvents this trap by concentrating on Rivière's text and that alone: the film "needed to be about the memoir and not about the crime," notes Foucault. Allio also asked peasants in a neighboring village to tell the story, and in spite of the 150 years that separated the crime and the film, it was "the same voices, the same accents, the same awkward and hoarse words, which recount the same barely transposed thing." The "economy" of Allio's cinemato-graphic choice, its "sparseness," allows one to gauge the "eternal present" of Rivière's case, what it is about it that continues on into the present.[60] This is both in terms of the villagers' grasp of a triple murder and in terms of the elusive account that upset systems of knowledge to the point where they were left speech-less, and which still paralyzes them today. Contemporary psychia-trists and criminologists continue "to share in the embarrassment of nineteenth-century psychiatrists, and have shown that they have nothing more to say."

These different examples from film are the proof: the search for a certain sobriety of images definitely guides Foucault's rela-tionship to film, to the extent that for him, what is specific to film is determined by this requirement for sparseness. The themes of film as an "art of poverty" (in a different way from the spe-cific case of Marguerite Duras in literature) also match up with different aspects of Foucault's work: *I, Pierre Rivière* and the archaeology of knowledges; *The Story of Paul* and strategies of power; *The Death of Maria Malibran* and "life as a work of art." We see a rejection of mimetic overstatement concerning his-torical reconstruction on one front and a condemnation of all Manicheism in the account of the effects of power on another. Yet elsewhere we see an asceticism in the representation of bod-ies that ensures a way out of the constraints of their organicity. In each case, a claim is made for what is specific to cinema, as the opposite side of the coin of what must be avoided, namely, embellishments, indeed any superfluity produced by the cam-era. This is why archaeological exploration rather than histori-cal illustration needs to be encouraged (*I, Pierre Rivière* vs. *Lacombe, Lucien*). The gray genealogy of relations of force rather than questionable representations of power relations is to be preferred (*The Story of Paul* vs. *The Night Porter*), and the difficult multiplication of bodies and pleasures rather than sentiments of love tried and tested a thousand times (Werner Schroeter vs. Ingmar Bergman).[61] We can see from this that if there is a positive specificity to film for Foucault, it's not to be found in an ontology of the image which seeks to respect the continuity of reality with a camera which has become "invisible" (as championed by André Bazin).[62] Neither is it a matter of bringing to light the immediate data of the image (such as movement in Deleuze).[63] Still less is it a question of approaching film in terms of a fact that is considered to be primary (like the narrative act in linguistic semiology). Rather, it is a matter of conceiving of a cinematic art relieved of any deliberately virtuoso exercise of its technical toolkit and of any aestheticizing approach ("retro" or otherwise) that claims to take the focus off the beaten path (at the same time as it sacralizes it). It's an art where a form of visual and aural asceticism leads to a dive into the arid maze of the archive, the difficulty of our relation to power, and the moving unknown of bodies.

CINEMA AND THE INTERVIEW

We still need to consider the situation of cinema in Foucault's writings and spoken words from a fresh angle. The determination of a cinematographic specificity expressed in the form of a requirement for "sparseness" allows us to resume an investigation into the "reappraisal" of knowledge through images. First, let's draw attention to an argumentative phenomenon that is clearly identifiable. This specificity is not given its own thematic status, even if it is formulated in different ways from one text to another. It would not be right, however, to see this lack of definition as an analytical failure and conclude that Foucault the archivist had no interest in the art of film. There is probably a solid reason that justifies the relatively modest place of film in Foucauldian production, especially in comparison with the pages he devoted to literature and painting in his work. This is quite apart from the idea that assumes that the philosopher had a predilection for a particular artistic practice. On this latter point, we would argue for the futility of an approach that took this study in the direction of biographical conjecture about a personal hierarchy of the arts in Foucault's work. This would include making a list of his favorite movies. Rather, we would argue that the fundamental reason for the modest place of film in his work has more to do with the conditions of possibility of the archaeological approach itself. This explains why Foucault didn't fully enter into the investigation of film in terms of what makes it unique and also explains at the same time why he didn't examine its integration with historical investigation in any detail. It's probably because the era that spawned cinema is not remote enough, and the archivist didn't have the necessary distance to describe effects and changes in the world of images. As Foucault writes in a famous passage in *The Archaeology of Knowledge*, "the analysis of the archive, then, involves a privileged region: at once close to us, and different from our present existence, it is the border of time that surrounds our presence, which overhangs it, and which indicates it in its otherness; it is that which, outside ourselves, delimits us."[64] It is in this sense that Foucault was able to explore the asylum, the clinic, or prison in the nineteenth century, mobilizing laws, internal regulations, treatises of anatomy, and so on, but also literary texts: so many statements (and visibilities) at the "border" of our present, and that the archivist could describe precisely because of the existence of this border that separates us from what we no longer are. We can understand, therefore, why Foucault's archaeological enterprise doesn't deal with the twentieth century, even if it is the difference between yesterday and today that allows the study of discontinuities: "The description of the archive deploys its possibilities . . . from what we can no longer say, and from that which falls outside our discursive practice."[65] Because film is a twentieth-century art, it doesn't have the same status as painting or literature. As Mathieu Potte-Bonneville has shown, painting and literature have a strong synthetic value for Foucault insofar as they "bring together the scattered traits of an era in the experience to which they bear witness": an era that is no longer our own and which we are in the process of leaving behind.[66]

For all the valuable insights into film Foucault provided in his interviews, "conversations," and newspaper articles, he didn't engage in a systematic reflection on the essence and forms of film's existence. This can be explained by the fact that the era during which film developed and acquired its artistic autonomy was not the subject of an archaeological examination and indeed, according to Foucault, couldn't be the subject of such an examination. The history of cinema simply isn't long enough; neither do we have enough temporal distance to describe its archives. This is in terms of the contexts we belong to and confront at either the local level (as Pasolini's "enquiry into sexuality" in Italy proves) or in terms of a recent history that still persists silently into the present (as evidenced by the "wall of silence" that was "erected around" the Second World War after 1945 in Germany, something that Syberberg seized on).[67] Nevertheless, if film wasn't called on as such by Foucault in his books, it's still the case that it served as a vehicle in the interviews for establishing a diagnosis of several aspects of contemporary history. In other words, when it came to moving images, the archivist's work continued in another way through the intermediary of that living and apparently improvised form of speech that is the interview. Deleuze draws attention really nicely to this double operation in Foucault's discourse in his books and interviews. On the one hand, you have a painstaking archaeological investigation that defines an institution in the past; on the other, you have the outline of an engagement with the present that never forces the reader to take a particular course of action. As Deleuze says:

> In most of his books he specifies a precise archive . . . regarding the General Hospital of the seventeenth century, the clinic of the eighteenth century, the prison of the nineteenth century, the subjectivity of Ancient Greece. . . . But that is one half of his task. For, through a concern for rigorousness, through a desire not to mix things up and through confidence in his reader, he does not formulate the other half. He formulates this explicitly only in the interviews which take place contemporary with the writing of each of his major books: what can be said nowadays about insanity, prison, sexuality? . . . [In interviews, Foucault] trace[d] these lines leading to the present which required a different form of expression from the lines which were drawn together in his major books. These *interviews are diagnostics.*[68]

There is no question that the interviews on film contribute to forging several diagnoses, connecting the dots to our current relationship to the Resistance in France, to internment in the asylum, to romantic conduct, and so on.

AN ATTEMPT TO REAPPRAISE KNOWLEDGE THROUGH FILM

The status of these written and spoken observations on film doesn't stop the archivist from problematizing his own era, even if he isn't able to describe it in full. We can now consider the other aspect of our investigation: not the epistemological status of discourse on film in relation to the rest of Foucault's work; rather, the possibility of a real encounter between film and the archive of an era. We have already partially addressed this point, noting with Foucault the need for a link between cinematic production and archaeological description, from the moment that it was clear that forms of knowledge were unable to examine certain past events, such as the Rivière case in 1836. In fact, the power of Allio's *I, Pierre Rivière* resides, among other things, in the continuity established between the peasants of the 1830s living in the village where the crime took place and the peasants living in a nearby village in the 1970s. The latter recaptured, almost with the same intonation, the sentences that were pronounced at the time when faced with the enigma of this triple murder. In a way, in setting up this impression of continuity from one century to another, the film takes on the challenge raised by Foucault's editorial project: namely, the challenge to systems of knowledge to make sense of Rivière's crime and to acknowledge this incomprehension if it still existed. "In the book we wanted to raise the question of Rivière again, and collect everything that had been said about Rivière at the time and after," says Foucault in "The Return of Pierre Rivière." The film's paradox is quite precisely making the failure to solve the enigma productive. "The Rivière enigma is by no means a lost cause, but the fact that it remains an enigma is not in vain, or without effects." That is, provided that the systems of knowledge—criminal medicine, psychiatry, criminology, etc.— made the effort to start over, that is, to call themselves into question after having "raise[d] the question of Rivière again."[69]

Thus film is able to "reappraise" systems of knowledge. It can also do this without having to deal with a remote period, as if the distance of an event in time was the only condition that allowed for a point of contact between knowledge and film. As we have seen, this link can also arise from a realization that relates to a historical moment closer to the archaeologist, as is evidenced in the interview "Film, History, and Popular Memory" and the films discussed (*Lacombe, Lucien, The Night Porter, The Sorrow and the Pity* [1969], and so on), which are all about the Second World War, in one way or another. According to Foucault, these different films raise a common problem, and in so doing they form a diagnosis of our relationship with this troubled period, without necessarily having a bird's-eye view of our present as our present ways of thinking and acting may still be a function of this period. Foucault formulates the problem in these terms: "Is it currently possible to make a *positive* film about the struggles of the Resistance?"[70] It's important to note that, beyond the visual (and aural) solutions, this statement is accompanied by an indication of a method that allows the links between film and archaeology to be strengthened. In the same interview, when asked about the persistent resentment that permeates films about political engagement during the Second World War (at the expense of showing struggles that didn't conform to the "retro" trend of the time), Foucault has this to say: "In my view, the politically important phenomenon lies in the phenomenon of the series rather than in any particular film. This is the network created by all these films and which, no pun intended, they occupy."[71] This leads to the question we mentioned before of a *positive* cinema of struggle, which synthesizes this phenomenon in the interrogative form. Using this approach, the phenomenon of the series sheds light on at least two points. First, it suggests the possibility of an archaeology that can be practiced in relation to problems that arise from film itself or from fragments of its history. The key concept in this passage is of course the "series." Foucault explains this in various places in his work, in particular in the introduction to *The Archaeology of Knowledge*, where there is a transition from a "total history" to a "general history." Total history is concerned with restoring "the overall form of a civilization, the principle—material or spiritual—of a society,"[72] and is on the lookout for a historicity arising from a causal explanation of all the transformations of that society, regardless of the variety of instances under consideration (economic, social, technical, political, and so on.) On the other hand, "general history" considers these aspects as so many "series," a word Foucault uses with a view to studying a whole system of "shifts" or "differences of level" between practices.[73] This is why "general history" is more sensitive to discontinuities and to what disrupts too great a linearity in the description of events. These events rely more on an ephemeral subject that changes with every era following the breaks that affect these events, rather than relying on a consciousness that believes itself to be the guardian of the cohesion of a period.[74]

If a "total" approach to history "draws all phenomena around a single centre—a principle, a meaning, a spirit, a world-view," in opposition—the "general" approach develops what Foucault calls a "space of dispersion," consisting precisely of "series" or more exactly "series of series," which he describes further as "tables."[75] Going back to the 1974 interview, "tables" can indeed be drawn up around film in dealing with a specifically historical problem, such as the problem of the depiction in film of a "positive" struggle relating to the Resistance. If we extend Foucault's thinking beyond the "Film, History, and Popular Memory" interview, it would appear that film lines up powerfully with the archaeological project, using its own mechanisms to elaborate a series and examination of an event that it is a part of, without becoming an arbitrary pretext for the archivist. A series is the proximity of one or more practices that problematize a fragment of history, and the event it refers back to remains unstable in itself, always difficult and elusive. Film is able to facilitate the understanding of a series, without seeking to freeze the inexhaustible nature of the event it harbors. How does Foucault see the event? A page from "The Order of Discourse" defines it clearly: history, far from turning away "from events: on the contrary . . . is constantly enlarging their field, discovering new layers of them, shallower or deeper. It is constantly isolating new sets of them, in which they are sometimes numerous, dense, and interchangeable, sometimes rare and decisive."[76] It's for this reason that the work of the archivist cannot be satisfied with a singular apprehension of the event or allow it to be subject to the rule of a uniform causality. This is what Foucault is saying when he refutes the idea that, after seeing Syberberg's *Hitler: A Film from Germany*, we can say, "This is what should have been done!" once and for all, about the war and the years that preceded it, precisely because "there is no *one* thing that should have been done about what happened between 1930 and 1945, there were a thousand, ten thousand, an infinite number of things that should have been done."[77] The multiple ways things can be filmed doesn't actually lead to a generalized relativism making them indistinguishable and erasing the density of the event being monitored. This multiplicity to which Foucault draws attention corresponds instead to the exigencies of a historical practice that seeks to constitute series around points of problematization that change our relationship to the past.[78] At the same time, these points appeal to the present to be on guard against any tendency toward amnesia. This is what Foucault means by "conveying a sense of history" or "intensifying parts of what we remember or what we've forgotten" in "The

Return of Pierre Rivière."[79] This is undoubtedly one of the most profound tasks of film.

Syberberg's entire filmography is about this, in that it seeks both to break and to represent the silence that had descended upon postwar Germany. Hence the question that he persists in asking, according to Foucault: "What has this become in the minds of Germans? What has this become in their hearts? What has this become in their bodies?"[80] Syberberg is not alone among German directors in raising this problem. Daney also cites the names of Thomas Harlan and Rainer W. Fassbinder in a text that tackles the relationship between the inglorious history of a country and the body of film that deals with it head on. These directors have known how to confront what French filmmakers struggled even to envisage, namely, a certain "work of mourning" in relation to a "grubby period of history," without escaping into retro or taking a moralizing overview. This is why French cinema "suffers from a quite exceptional deficit of memory," as is evidenced by the yawn-inducing *Uranus* (1990).[81] It might be better "meditate on" the German case, where the aforementioned filmmakers, each in his own way, have experimented with the idea that film is an art that "oscillates" between yesterday and today, ensuring by means of this experimentation that the "past moves on" even if just a little. Thus a series of films dealing with the legacy of Nazism in Germany has emerged independently of the diversity of positions occupied by these directors in the history of film in their country (or perhaps it is due to this very diversity). To return to Syberberg, how does he resolve the question of this legacy? What layers of this event does he uncover that might allow the way in which a historical moment continued to persist in the Germany of the 1970s and 1980s to be perceived? For Foucault, the power of *Hitler: A Film from Germany* resides in its capacity to make one feel the everyday abjection of Nazism; not just the horror of the regime with its countless massacres and infernal propaganda machine (although these are both called to account in the film), but what is despicable in the most ordinary of things—clothing, popular culture, ways of talking, and so on. Obviously Syberberg is not content just to simply reconstruct this everyday ignominy; he goes much further: he raises it to a higher level of expression that prevents any empathy on the part of the viewer, while maintaining the power of fascination that this everyday horror was able to exercise at the time. This is what makes this film, according to Foucault, a "beautiful monster" insofar as Syberberg "has managed to bring out a certain beauty in this history without concealing what was sordid, ignoble, and mundanely abject about it. It is here, perhaps, where he has grasped Nazism at its most seductive, a certain intensity of abjection, a certain sparkle of mediocrity, which was doubtless one of Nazism's powers of enchantment."[82] Foucault had already drawn attention in the "Film, History, and Popular Memory" interview to one of the aspects that made Malle's *Lacombe, Lucien* "interesting." The film shows that the "most intoxicating" part of dictatorship was not based on the possession of power by one man, whom everybody identified with, experiencing a certain pleasure through this identification. Rather, the intoxication in question was more a matter of "the fact that a part of the power was actually delegated to a certain fringe of the masses," and "this kind of regime [Nazism] gave the most dreadful, but in a sense the most intoxicating, part of power to a considerable number of people." Even *The Night Porter* poses a similar problem, that of the "*love for power.*"[83]

We thus return to the theme of the eroticization of power, which we discussed at the beginning of this study, and whose slogan "in the current context," as Foucault put it in 1974, is

"Love me, because I am power." Syberberg takes up this theme in another way and in a more nuanced manner than Malle and Cavani, whose films are not exempt from a form of the banalization of horror. The German filmmaker tries to show instead that "horror is banal, that banality contains dimensions of horror within itself." We need to compare Syberberg's films with Fassbinder's (for example, *The Marriage of Maria Braun* [1979]) and possibly with Werner Herzog's, whose films Foucault liked, then analyze in turn the network created by their respective works in relation to a common historical heritage. This is a way of linking film to archival work, even if it means connecting to another heterogeneous series in a field beyond that of moving images: a series of series that forms the web of problematizations that marks our time. Philosophy can be a part of this if it addresses the question of the eroticization of power on its own ground, as is the case in *Anti-Oedipus*, the book coauthored by Gilles Deleuze and Félix Guattari in 1972. Foucault wrote a preface for the 1977 edition, the year Syberberg made *Hitler: A Film from Germany*. In this text, Foucault describes *Anti-Oedipus* as a manual on the art of living, "a guide to everyday life," or more precisely as an *"Introduction to the Non-Fascist Life."* In fact, one of the rules for living contained therein can be formulated in this way: "Do not become enamored of power"; in any case, a saving humor runs throughout. As he says: "The book often leads one to believe it is all fun and games, when something essential is taking place, something of extreme seriousness: the tracking down of all varieties of fascism, from the enormous ones that surround and crush us to the petty ones that constitute the tyrannical bitterness of our everyday lives."[84] Film and philosophy deal with the same problem differently, and several distinct series intersect in the gap between them. Moving images, just as much as conceptual elements, paint a picture of a general history of this love for power that has fed the fascisms of the past and continues to envelope those of the present.

At the end of this journey, it would seem that the presence of Foucault's archaeological approach in his texts on film is much more obvious than a first reading might suggest. In this sense, cinema's reappraisal of knowledge doesn't remain simply at the level of mere intentions; it is effective even if it is scattered throughout the interviews. We have tried to show how the status of Foucault's "words and writings"[85] is especially suited to the examination of film, and that, strictly speaking, they could become a more legitimate site for a diagnosis of our present than the books. It's not simply a question of reassessing the role of film in the disciplines of knowledge by pointing out that film occupies a real place at the level of visibilities, which is the other pole of Foucault's archaeological description of statements. In other words, it's not simply a matter of considering films to be a part of what Deleuze described as an "audiovisual archive" in his monograph on the philosopher.[86] Rather, it's a matter of taking into account the operations of thought that relate to historical inquiry in Foucault's work and understanding how these permeate his interviews and conversations on film. At the same time, these operations open up the possibility for contemporary applications by historians, philosophers, or cinephiles (or someone who is all three).

To conclude, and to hand over the virtual task of continuing this investigation through film, what elements of Foucauldian archaeology can be transferred into the world of film? We saw these elements in Allio's *I, Pierre Rivière*, and we have just seen them in Syberberg's *Hitler: A Film from Germany*. We have seen the establishment of the phenomenon of *series*: probing certain events in history, and problematizing both our degree of participation in those events and our ability to act. In one instance, we have

the memory of popular struggle, and in another, the eroticization of power. Flowing on from this, of course, is an interest in
breaks in history, while not forgetting the attention Foucault
brings to what he terms in *The Archaeology of Knowledge* as "singular forms of *persistence*," those strange continuities that constitute an "eternal present" through the ages, including the most
everyday actions and reactions, as Allio shows in his film on
Rivière.[87] Indeed, the *everyday* is another notion associated with
the archivist's practice, persisting through several interviews. As
we have seen, the everyday has little to do with common sense,
let alone an improbable good sense. Instead, it corresponds to
this whole patchwork assembly of miniscule events, necessitat-
ing what Foucault describes in "The Order of Discourse" as
"pushing to its extreme the fine grain of the event,"[88] and what
he also called the "miniscule grain of history," an expression that
Allio liked citing. Foucault proposed a film-related synonym
for this, referring to Antonioni: "It's like *Blow-Up* if you like, a
kind of explosion that is produced in all ventures of this kind,
just as in daily life," before adding: "That's what the Rivière
case is like, and it's that what the film shows: daily life, a dispute over a field, furniture, old clothes."[89] The emergence of discontinuities in history sometimes depends on these tiny events
that film, that art of the infinitely small, is able to reveal or at
least is capable of revealing (as Jean Epstein and other great pioneers understood right at the outset of the invention of film).
Film, when not contaminated by the "fashion for retro," is also
capable of transforming anonymous figures from the past into
historical characters (but not into heroes). Following on from
the previous point, film shares with archaeology the same concern with *description*. Foucault responds soberly to those who
reproached René Féret in *The Story of Paul* for restricting himself
to a description of asylum internment and nothing else, saying:

"You know, I think describing is already something important."[90] Description is inseparable from an apprehension of the effects of power and a perception of the forces in the frustrating relationships that bind us to institutions in general and to the strategies they deploy. Deleuze often praised the descriptive power of Foucault's writing as being inseparable from a higher vision. As Deleuze affirmed in an interview contemporary with his book *Time-Image*, "In a way, he was a kind of *seer*. And what he saw was actually intolerable. He was a fantastic seer. It was the way he saw people, the way he saw everything, in its comedy and misery."[91] According to Foucault, the fact that film has been endowed with a capacity for description similar to that of other practices (discursive or otherwise) finally allows film to act as a "cross-check" against time.

2

VERSIONS OF THE PRESENT

Foucault's Metaphysics of the Event
Illuminated by Cinema

PATRICE MANIGLIER

oucault wrote no books on film. He barely even mentioned
film. One senses an embarrassment, a reserve, and sometimes a frank admission of incompetence in the few interviews we have from him on the subject. But perhaps it is this
reserve, this timidity, that is valuable to us today. It prevented
Foucault from providing an overview of film from which philosophy could pronounce the truth on it as one object among
others, displayed under the eye of the sovereign concept. Foucault had nothing to say *about* cinema as an object to be quali-
fied.[1] So there's no sense in thinking about a possible "encounter"
between Foucault and film if we want to discover any solid
essential truths about this art (this technique and this mystery,
to quote Godard.)[2] But for all this, there was an encounter. Even
if it was inchoate, incomplete, incidental, almost anecdotal,
fragmented, and one-sided, something happened that was not
without interest.

Admittedly, it wasn't Foucault who went to the movies, but
it was the movies that came to Foucault, through the questions
of a number of critics and directors. The one exception to this
appears to be his meeting with Werner Schroeter, which he himself solicited.[3] But even there, one finds nothing that compares

to the magnificent texts that Foucault wrote on painting or literature, works in their own right. Cinema had done more reading of Foucault's books than the latter had done of the films he saw. But it's not a truth about itself that film sought in Foucault. Instead, it sought instruments to address the *problems* that it dealt with: relationships to the past, to politics, sexuality, madness, and the body. It would be a mistake, however, to see common "themes" between what Foucault was writing about and what certain films were dealing with at the same time. In the same way that film isn't a subject for the philosopher, there's little to be gained by comparing the objects of madness, sexuality, the body, the memory of popular struggles as they appear in Foucault's words with these objects as they appear in the films of Féret, Pasolini, Schroeter, and Allio. These were *problems* that were raised equally for everyone, regardless of their field.

What characterizes a problem is that it always questions the legitimacy of the questioning that underlies it. Philosophy doesn't discuss sexuality, madness, or the body or the past without needing to reexamine both what it means to speak, and whether it is appropriate to speak of madness and sexuality and so on. In the same way, film doesn't display the past, madness, or sex without having to question not only its own means and methods but also the very existence of what it is supposed to "display." Sexuality is not a problem in the sense that it bothers us, embarrasses us, or largely escapes our understanding. It only becomes a problem when we are no longer sure that something exists that needs to be examined, that is, when it challenges the question. A problem, therefore, appears only when an object starts to falter, when the object can no longer maintain its distance as something we can elucidate with instruments that already exist. The assumptions with which we approach the object are destabilized, right down to the identity of the subject who is doing the questioning.

These are the conditions of a true *encounter*: practices of thought never encounter each other except around problems.[4] And it is in this sense that there was indeed an encounter between Foucault and film. In particular, it is in these terms that the critics of *Cahiers du cinéma* formulated Foucault's excursion into history. They presented it as a "path" for an analogous excursion into the genre of the historical film (and more generally the political or militant genre). In the field where Foucault was operating, something similar was playing out in what others wanted to do on the screen. We need to say something about how, and on what terms, and to what purpose this exemplarity of the Foucauldian approach to film was effected and what cinema can expect to bring into its own domain of the Foucauldian *action* on history. But the most important question we want to ask here is a question on the rebound: not so much what film was able to do with Foucault, but more, what Foucault *could have* done with film. It's about seeing how this encounter sought out by film might illuminate the problems that Foucault himself asked. Foucault revolutionizes history, Paul Veyne wrote proudly at the same time as many of these interviews on film were being conducted.[5] Our question is simple: does the fact that film felt that this revolution was relevant to itself, and that a revolution of the same type could and should be effected in film, tell us something about this question?

We are not looking to cover the entirety of the encounter between Foucault and film, as if we could imagine a kind of deductive system, which would allow us to reconstruct all the problems Foucault shared with film in these very brief and fragmented moments (insanity, the asylum, and sexual identity with Féret, sexuality with Pasolini, the nature of Nazism with Syberberg and the body with Schroeter, and so on). The focus will be on a quite particular problem, which seems to us to be at the very heart of Foucault's own approach: that is, the problem of the event, the relation to the past and what makes history. But it is only with a renewed reserve and a renewed timidity that we will approach this question. Because it is not a matter of showing either what film can learn from Foucault's historical practice or what Foucault's genealogical or archaeological approach can learn from the efforts of film to solve analogous problems in its own domain. The reason for this is simple: I am not a filmmaker, historian, or even a film critic. My question is slightly different. I will ask how this encounter might transform, not the practice of various parties, but rather the understanding of the philosophical issues these practices raise. It so happens that the displacements that Foucault imposes in relation to historical method raise eminently philosophical questions. History cannot be done differently without the total disruption of fundamental insights concerning the nature of time, the relation of the past and the present, the event, human action, and the way subjects are situated in both the natural and cultural worlds. Foucault doesn't revolutionize history without obliging us to reinvent philosophy.

Foucault was obviously the first to know this and continually insisted on the philosophical stakes of his own approach. Hence, in his very fine text in 1971 on "Nietzsche, Genealogy, History," he writes that "effective history" is not so much about the search for continuities between past and present and beyond, or explanations about the situation we are in or what we were and what we did in other segments of the timeline. Rather "effective history" is about the quest for a discontinuity, a passion for differences, for everything specifically that makes us

differ from what we were; it is a quest for all those accidents
that have torn us from our imaginary destinies in a way that was
no more foreseeable than it is retroactively explainable today.[6]
From this follows a whole dislocation of time, where time is no
longer that element in which individual and collective beings
bathe and transform and become what they are, but rather the
empty space where a worrying disconnection of singular and random "events" emerges. "The true historical sense confirms our
existence among countless lost events, without a landmark or a
point of reference."[7] So, what is this "totally different form of
time,"[8] this time that no longer unites past, present, and future?
What is this jagged surface where events appear without following on from each other? And what is this part of our "being"
where, according to Foucault, genealogy introduces discontinuity?[9] Isn't this quite clearly far removed from what philosophers
call "substance," this element of thingness that persists through
its own transformations, like the individual, Socrates, when he
is sitting and when he is standing? What do we have to be in
order to be the subject of genealogy? These are the questions we
would like to address while offering the hypothesis that a focus
on a number of films can allow us to develop these questions
better and perhaps to answer them better as well.

It's clear that these questions are not just methodological. It's
not simply a matter of knowing how to reconstruct the past
correctly, or what should be preserved as documents; nor is
it about knowing how to interpret traces and determine what
causalities are valid (social, economic, ideological, and political),
and so on. The questions genealogy raises are, in fact, *metaphysical* questions: they concern the very essence of what we are
talking about, they force us to reexamine the most basic conceptual frameworks that guide historians. What is an event? What
is time? What is the past? What is the present? Genealogy

cannot "historicize" what we thought was eternal, reintroducing, as Foucault says, "within a process of development everything considered immortal in man,"[10] without the term "history" itself becoming mysterious once more. If Foucault revolutionizes history, it's so that we might no longer know what it means to be in history or to make history. The radicalism of this revolution can be grasped only if one perceives the metaphysical dimension.

It is perhaps surprising to see such a worthy, well-worn, almost arthritic term applied to the critical, skeptical, relativist, and engaged thought of Michel Foucault. It's hard to imagine metaphysicians in togas demonstrating with the Groupe d'Information sur les Prisons.[11] It's hard to imagine the speculative thinker agreeing with Foucault that we shouldn't hesitate to start a fight with the police because that's what cops are made for, namely, physical violence.[12] Besides, isn't metaphysics the declared enemy of Nietzschean genealogy? But it's only a question of words here. If we describe metaphysics as a certain conception of thought that defines it as a meditation on the eternal questions and a certain idea of Being that defines it as a kind of invariance and necessity that thought alone, by its own means (those, say, of "pure reason"), can establish beyond the variability and contingency of events, then, indeed, it is not a question of metaphysics. But then how do we describe the questioning of these basic notions? We propose to define metaphysics more simply as the best exercise for elaborating on that wonder when we are faced with what is most familiar to us and which seems to be what is most necessary to our understanding of the world. Metaphysics is not about dealing with the most elevated and most obscure of questions (the soul, the world, God, eternity, and so on); instead it deals with the simplest questions: what is a thing, an event, a cause, an effect, time, a relationship, an action, an agent? From this point of view, we can say that Foucault's practice is continually accompanied by a metaphysics.

What is of interest to us here, therefore, is the metaphysics of Foucault's historical approach and the way it can be better elaborated if it is compared to certain operations that take place in film. It's not a matter of comparing history in general with film in general. René Allio and Alain Resnais are no more the embodiment of film than Foucault is of history. What we see in film are creations, acts, singular operations effected in a medium that is, of course, characterized both by its technical forms and by its artistic heritage. These operations form not an essence but an unstable situation, a set of open possibilities, which can be taken up (or not), and which can be manipulated (sometimes for the worse), in short, what Foucault himself calls fields of discursive and nondiscursive *practice*.[13] In the films we mention, we won't be looking for some revelation about the essence of the medium of film, but instead for uses, shifts, and suggestions. Neither is it a matter of discovering what film in general can tell us about history in general, but rather of seeing how creative singularities illuminate each other precisely because, in not actualizing themselves through the same subject matter, or in the same field, their comparison allows for the extraction of something like the abstract operation that takes place in each of them, the pure action that characterizes them. The *generic* issues that are specific to them can't be drawn out except through this confrontation.[14] It is not far-fetched to say that thinking only ever draws its generic dimension from a singularity. In this sense, we will try to let the historical-critical practices of Foucault and film reflect on each other.

PORTRAIT OF FOUCAULT AS A METAPHYSICIAN

A History Without Substance: From "the Memory of Popular Struggles"
to the Metaphysics of the Event

The interview in *Cahiers du cinéma* that we will be beginning
with seems far removed from the metaphysical considerations
we would like to link it to.[15] Rather, it appears to deal with
issues that were very topical at the time, namely, the representation of the period of the Occupation and Resistance in film in
the mid-1970s in France. The critics of the *Cahiers* spotted what
was, in their view, a biased rewriting of the history of this
period, through what they termed a "fashion for retro." Illus-
trated particularly by Louis Malle's film *Lacombe, Lucien* (1974),
the result of this biased rewriting was to deny subjects all intelligence and all initiative in relation to their own history on the
pretext of demystifying the heroic memory of the Resistance
carefully maintained by Gaullist power. This ended up sending
out a message that there never was any struggle; we were all
either "spineless layabouts"[16] or the "pawns of history,"[17] and
probably both at the same time. They also noticed in this an
imposition on the contemporary audience, which not only erased
a part of their history but also made them doubt the very possibility of there having been subjects of resistance. But it was
not a question, of course, for Daney, Toubiana, and Bonitzer, of
defending the Gaullist episode. The ideological functions (the
justification of de Gaulle's personal power and policies in the
name of a very specific state nationalism) and historical distor-
tions (the myth of the separation of the history of Vichy from
the history of the French state) of this episode were equally
obvious. The question was rather: Was it possible to maintain
something like a memory of the struggles without falling back

into Gaullist heroization? Was a different story of the Resistance possible, which might circumvent the interpretation that made it naturally tend toward the establishment of a certain political, nationalist, state, consensual, and ultimately repressive power? Could it be restored to a history that, in the spirit of the writers of the *Cahiers* of this period, was probably more in continuity with the revolutionary struggles of the 1960s and insurrectional movements in France in the 1970s? Nonetheless, one senses a certain hesitation here: Daney, Toubiana, and Bonitzer were not so much seeking to enlist the memory of the Resistance in another *cause* as to suspend these teleological rereadings of history for a moment. It was not about opposing the idea that the Resistance was conducted in the name of "a certain idea of France," the idea that it was really fighting for a society delivered from exploitation, a hope that was betrayed at the moment of the Liberation. Rather, it was more about focusing on what might have been a memory of popular struggles from the perspective of those who were involved before the meaning of these struggles was, as it were, hijacked by the grand apologist narratives justifying whatever powers were in place.[18] It was true that history, even at its most violent, and in particular this history, the history of the Resistance, was made (perhaps not exclusively, but primarily) by those who didn't gain any extra power from it, even when they were on the winning side. History was made by the "dominated," the "governed," the "exploited." It was therefore a matter of resisting two ideas equally: that the masses were apathetic or complicit, and that they acted for a cause that was already established.

Foucault shares the conviction that history is an ideological affair with his interviewers; that memory is a terrain of struggles and film is one of the sites where this struggle is waged. This latter site differs from others (the history of historians, literature, journalism, etc.), only quantitatively through the power of its effects: "Nowadays cheap literature is no longer enough. There are the much more effective means of television and film. And I think this is a way of *reencoding* popular memory, which still exists but is unable to find an expression. So people are shown, not what they actually were, but what they need to remember themselves as having been."[19] Memory is thus a process of rewriting traces of traces but is immediately divided into two essentially uneven regimes of traces, dominant traces and dominated traces, official history and popular memory. The question then becomes whether the difference between these traces is only a matter of degree (the former being simply more visible than the latter) or perhaps it is mainly a difference of nature (memory doesn't function as history). Correspondingly, it becomes a question of whether the challenge is simply to replace a false and fabricated history with a true and authentic history that somehow doesn't impose a false version of the past on those who lived it. Or is it simply a matter of accepting a version of the past that hasn't been "formulated" because it expresses the point of view of those who do not have political, economic, or cultural power? Is it a matter perhaps of a totally different relation to the past, which is not situated at the same level as the other? Finally, one might wonder whether film is not a more or less powerful medium in this struggle, or if it has a specificity that allows it to achieve singular effects, to which writing cannot accede.

It seems that, for Foucault, "popular memory" is not just another voice, simply less heard than the others, one that doesn't carry as far, drowned out, as it were, by the loudspeakers of official ideology. Instead, it is another way of speaking. Between these two memories there is a formal, therefore qualitative, difference, not just a quantitative one. To the question "of how to produce a new type of hero, a positive hero," Foucault responds: "The problem is not the hero, but the struggle. Can a film be made about struggle without the traditional processes of heroization? We are coming back to an old problem here: how has history come to engage in the discourse that it has and to exploit what has happened, other than through the epic, and by offering itself as a story of heroes? That's how the history of the French Revolution has been written. Film has proceeded in the same fashion. This can always be contrasted with its ironic flip side: 'No, look, there are no heroes. We're all swine, and so on.'"[20] But what might a history that wasn't the history of a hero (or a swine) look like? What might a history that had broken with the epic pattern look like? It would be a history that wouldn't recount the constitution of a self. It wouldn't say: "See how we've struggled to become what we are." It wouldn't seek out the record of its costly birth in the past. Foucault says with great precision that it wouldn't even try to "salvage" the past. A strange history this, that doesn't try to persist beyond its actual disappearance. It would indeed speak of struggles, but it wouldn't attribute them to a subject, as if history were one grand gesture, a series of memorable actions that show what an agent is capable of. Epic history, for its part, must always attribute the battle, the struggles, to a subject who takes on a part in a conflict, the nation, the people, a class, and is organized through this *continuity* between past and present. But what characterizes popular memory, according to Foucault, is a certain withdrawal from historical unity, and a certain molecularization. *Struggles*: not the history *of* something, *of* someone. Instead of a large entity that spans different vagaries, we have lines that escape all attribution to a historical subject and to a living whole. The "people" is not another substance of historical life (different from "elites"); it is, on the contrary, what removes history from any totalizing substance. In this sense, the people has no history. The traces of popular struggles render the history of nations and classes porous, they take away its calm division into periods ("first there was this, then there was that"). It is quite the opposite of a de Gaulle writing that we are part of that great entity, France, and that we will continue on reasonably well in that mode. Popular struggles don't belong to anyone: they follow a set of threads that are constantly rewoven but are not written into history, have never been written, and never will be written. They disrupt history rather than having a history. History is the way in which substantive totalization claims to overcome these disruptions in order to make of these accidents a moment in its own life.

Popular history is characterized by the fact that it is not attributable to anything: it is, as Louis Althusser saw so well, a *process without a subject*.[21] This is why it can't take the form of the hero's epic. The people are not the French; neither are they the workers or the peasants. If they were, then there would be another history, for example, that of the working class acceding to the conquest of its own essence, power—or perhaps even its defeat. But then this would be official history again. The people are traitors: they can be found in history, but like a virus. They haunt our history, but our history is not theirs, no matter who we are otherwise (dominators or dominated). What characterizes *minority* memory is precisely that it is not the history of a being who is either already formed or in the process of formation. In reality, every majority history is told from the end, as an already completed history, one that has an already formed horizon.[22] For its part, popular memory couldn't care less about being formed. It is these processes that defy any identification.

If popular memory is defined by the fact that it cannot speak for itself, it's not because its voice is not loud enough, it's simply because it doesn't have a self. Whoever speaks for themselves already speaks for another. Popular memory is not just another point of view on a set of conflicting relations declared by a party that the judge doesn't hear from often. It is the dimension of becoming that doesn't claim a point of view, and which is not a matter of recognition, because it doesn't recognize the trial that has been set up in advance to bring the points of view into confrontation. It doesn't prefigure the existence of a well-defined space where what happens, happens, where we can discuss what happened to *us*. It doesn't accept this "us," not through any particular inhumanity but because it doesn't need to: it doesn't conspire with an "us" but falls short of any kind of "us." It organizes lateral communications with other becomings that are not chronological or spatial. Popular struggles in twentieth century France are not part of the history of France; instead, they are among the things that happened, those which quite specifically threaten the identity of the subjects composed by that history.

This doesn't mean, of course, that popular struggles belong to a kind of eternity, where everything is in communication with everything else, a kind of background to the whole of human history, which emerges occasionally, is stifled, but is never extinguished. Such a background would still be a substance. It doesn't mean that nothing ever changes, that all of history is nothing but the ever precarious forms taken by attempts to silence this endless battle of sightless underground moles struggling without end or purpose, while a few sparks erupt every now and then from the depths of the ageless magma of human agitation. Instead, what it does mean is that there are events that, strictly speaking, don't belong to history. They are becomings without an underlying substance, changes that don't occur in chronological time because they are not the passage of one state of affairs to another. We can see that this is a strictly metaphysical issue: how do you think about becomings without thinking about it as the constitution or evolution of a thing endowed with an identity (a nation, an individual, even humanity as a whole)—in short as events without substance? But it is not only in relation to the memory of popular struggles that Foucault encounters this question. We will now see that it informs his entire work.

History as Critique: An Introduction to the Event—Concept Number 1

Nothing would be more misleading than to view Foucault's interest in objects that are seemingly "minor" (in every sense of the term), namely, the mad, the sick, prisoners, sexual perverts, and so on, as an attempt to expand our historical memory to objects hitherto rejected by official history, or to view this interest as a means of atoning for the way history continues to exercise violence against a section of humanity in the present by reinforcing through amnesia the distinction between who is worthy of interest (the elite) and who is insignificant (the people). Such an approach would imply a wish to transfer official history's scheme of intelligibility to its margins. It would be aimed at showing how significant the existence of ordinary people was in reality and reintegrating those who had been rejected by the vast adventure of humanity and our culture in the process of maintaining social hierarchies.[23] But in doing this we would be failing to examine the actual form of this knowledge, the processes by which we give meaning to the past. Foucault constantly insists that in madness, in the prison, in "subjugated knowledges"[24] we need to look not just for a new object for a history that is already sure of itself, of its legitimacy and the ways it is exercised; rather, we need a critical tool against this history. What is required is an analysis of the displacements, torsions, exclusions, and eradications that are required to turn ourselves into subjects of knowledge. In the preface to *History of Madness*, Foucault writes that madness cannot be an object of history; it is a challenge to history.[25] In the same way, at around the same time he was being interviewed by *Cahiers du cinéma*, he explained in a wonderful article titled "Lives of Infamous Men," intended as an introduction to a series of books that never eventuated, that the project was not justified by a concern for giving people who had been removed from the public existence and collective memory during their lifetimes the glory (*fama*) they deserved, simply through the mere fact of their existence, as if everything deserved to be said, simply because they had gone to the trouble of being born.[26] On the contrary, the project was justified on the basis that these lives had passed into language without being composed as objects due to the manner in which they were recorded. Indeed, the words by which they come to us are the very words that needed to be spoken in order to silence them, to shut them up in asylums, to remove them from interaction with others so that ordinary life could continue in the silence of their collective voices. These traces were not testimony but deletions, "an effacement of the thing said by its very utterance."[27] But in this process, something from the past comes through language, not so much as an object but as a *force* that had to be minimized with just enough language to make it disappear. Thus Foucault says that these lives are not there in terms of the meaning of these words but there as pure effects, a kind of pure energy that is not objectified through language, because it's a means to applying the force necessary for the perpetuation of the way the significant and insignificant are divided. "*Exempla*, but unlike those collected by the sages in the course of their readings, they are examples that convey not so much lessons to ponder as brief effects whose force fades almost at once."[28] We can see yet again that it's not about extending the shadow of legend beyond objects considered worthy of attention but rather of finding a nonlegendary relationship to the past. For Foucault, here as elsewhere, the relationship to the past is not directed against forgetting but against history itself. It's about relating to becoming in a nonhistorical manner.

If we look at all his work we can verify that for Foucault, the past has never been the *object* of an already established knowledge, but instead it is the instrument of a *critique* of the present. History for him is never a positivist discipline among others but always a new form of what Kant called critique.[29] The objective of critique, in the Kantian sense, is to uncover the assumptions that form us, and in particular, those that organize us as subjects of knowledge. In contradistinction to Kant, Foucault is not searching for the assumptions that underlie all knowledge, in an a priori reflection on the conditions that allow us to make a legitimate claim to some kind of objective knowledge. He is interested instead in a form of knowledge that is able to redefine the subject by the way it differs from its object, that is, by all the ways in which it is not (or no longer) its object. History is one such form of knowledge.[30] Its task is not to establish the past or to explain the present but, on the contrary, to allow us to redefine ourselves (which includes as historical subjects) by the whole set of differences and displacements through which we have ceased to be what we were. Thus the history of madness is not the history of a thing whose existence cannot be doubted (the unreasonable behavior of some humans), or even the history of opinions about these behaviors, but the history—can we still call it that?—of the necessary shifts, maneuvers, and real transformations that took place in order for madness to appear quite specifically as a problem and therefore be made the object of a history. It is thus from the "other," from the past, that we ask for the measure of our identity. We are nothing other than a variant of what we were, and we must define ourselves by all the differences that form us. So instead of critique assuring us of our right to establish truths about an objective world, it serves instead to reveal the contingency of this very right.

This critical conception of history explains, I think, the very particular status the past has for Foucault. Genealogy doesn't relate to the past as a proven objective fact but as a *variant*, against which the present can test its own contingency, that is, the always open possibility it can *be other*. In the same way, anthropologists are not looking for objects to be known in distant cultures but alternative versions that allow them to relativize anthropology itself.[31] In short, for the genealogist, the past is another possible self, an interior difference that allows identity to be undone, or rather, for it to be redefined specifically through difference. The prescription "to get free of oneself" in the introduction to *The Use of Pleasure* is valid for all Foucault's work, right from the beginning.[32] And it needs to be understood in the same way as Lévi-Strauss's definition of anthropology as "a technique of estrangement."[33] The present doesn't relate to the past in terms of one thing succeeding another along the continuous line of time but as a variant defining itself exclusively by the sum of its differences from other variants.

This undoubtedly implies a very profoundly relativistic conception. But here again we must avoid a misunderstanding. Foucault can extend the historical approach to new objects that were once believed to be timeless only by reopening the question of the kind of being or, if you like, the regime of objectivity, that is change. It's not just a matter of saying that certain things we thought eternal are actually historical—for example, that we have a sexuality, that there are mad people, that we have to punish, that we are subjects, that man exists, or indeed that everything is historical and so on. Instead, it's about showing that the whole notion of the being of the past can be thrown into question. Actually, it is not enough to suggest that all eternal truths should be "historically relativized" and to banish our certainties to the dates and locations of their conditions of emergence. To do this would be to put in place an even more powerful invariant, an even more all-encompassing point of reference: that is, the very notion of history itself. This alleged historical relativism is nothing more than a new dogmatism. Instead of judging human life against strong scientific or moral truths, everything is measured against one truth, namely, that of history, a truth that is barely questioned. One could say, for example: "Newtonian physics is not the inscription of a natural reality that has finally been revealed on the screen of human consciousness, but simply a human creation, dependent and even reducible to the context in which it was born. Physics is the product of its time, Nature itself is a historical notion." But en route we have established a new ultimate frame of reference: that of an active and suffering humanity, unfolding in time, stretching along a thin one-dimensional line, measured in hours, days, months, years, centuries, perhaps fragmented into watertight groups called societies, which group together to form that object we call history, this "science of men in time," as Marc Bloch defines it.[34]

Genealogy rejects this, precisely because in terms of method, decision, and hypothesis, it's not about establishing objective truths but about testing all absolutes and subjecting all invariants to variation. Foucault explains this clearly in his article on Nietzsche: the history of historians, insofar as it places its objects in the global repository of time "reintroduces (and always assumes) a suprahistorical perspective." The "historical sense" consists precisely in leaving nothing outside change: it "can evade metaphysics and become a privileged instrument of genealogy if it refuses the certainty of absolutes."[35] Genealogy doesn't relativize things according to a fixed point of reference (chronological time) but relativizes the points of reference themselves (including the calendar) in their reciprocal intertwining. Things don't need to be engulfed in a set of global points of reference because we are able to define the identity of each point of reference *intrinsically* by their mutual differences and not with reference to the state of the overall situation of the world at such and such a point of time. Making invariants variant, relativizing absolutes, even those we have set up as points of reference (humanity, reason, health, the body, and so on) and exposing the contingency of necessities we believe to be nonnegotiable demonstrates the shifts, shows of force, side steps, tensions, and reinterpretations needed to make the points of reference that we use seem so natural. More accurately, it demonstrates that these variants can be defined only through these shifts. But this critical attitude implies a renunciation of our instinctive conception of change as the passage of one thing to another *in* time. Where history sets up its grand chronological table of references with its dates and years, and can only do so by making each event a modification of the total state of a transformable present, genealogy "leaves nothing around the self, deprives the self of the reassuring stability of life and nature." This "differs from the history of historians in being without constants. Nothing in man—not even his body—is sufficiently stable to serve as the basis for self-recognition or for understanding other men."[36] So it must give up both the idea of substance (or ontological continuity) and the idea of succession. An event is not a transition that leads a thing from one state (defined by a certain number of properties or a certain composition of elements) to another (different properties or different combinations) against the abstract and empty backdrop of time.

This brings us back to the point that the event cannot be defined as the modification *of* something (of a substance), as it's everything (the whole present) that needs to be defined as an event. So we can see how Foucault's *critical* practice of history necessarily intersects with rather vertiginous philosophical questions, for example, events that come to nothing but subsist in themselves, such as Alice's "smile without a cat," which Gilles Deleuze saw as the model for the event.[37] There is also a time that is not of the order of succession, a nonchronological time, where presents don't succeed each other on a line measured in countable units but relate to each other as mirror images of each other, like the facets of a single crystal made out of two-way mirrors. There are identities that consist of nothing but their difference from others (variants). Foucault very simply said as much in his inaugural lecture at the Collège de France: "This analysis poses philosophical, or theoretical, problems, and very likely formidable ones. . . . [W]hat status must be given to that notion of event?"[38] He suggested some elements of a response to this question that clearly alluded to the philosophy developed a few years earlier by Deleuze in *The Logic of Sense*,[39] on which he himself had provided a commentary. The event, he said, calls for a "materialism of the incorporeal," "it is not the act or the property of a body" but "consists in the relation, the coexistence, the dispersion, overlapping, the accumulation, and the selection of material elements."[40]

The most systematic attempt Foucault made to both practically and "theoretically" explore such an ontology of the event can be seen in *The Archaeology of Knowledge*.[41] This ontology doesn't fall from the sky of eternal truths where Foucault, in company with his friend Deleuze, might have gone to steal it, like new Prometheuses stealing fire from the gods. It simply tries to take stock of the deformations of the ordinary or traditional concept of the event produced by the critical practice of history that Foucault had undertaken in his previous works. In short, this ontology is a diagnosis of the effects of the conceptual shift that his own historical approach produces in understanding the concepts it manipulates. The question of what Foucault's view of the event is is thus inseparable from the question of how Foucault goes about extracting events from historical data, that is, from the corpus.

To brutally cut short what is running the risk of becoming a very long demonstration, let's just say that an event can be defined as *a nondeductive system of homologous gaps in heterogeneous series*. To reconstruct an event, a series must first be established.[42] A series is a set of terms that follow on from another in such a way that relationships of ordered transformations can be established and in such a way that one term appears as the repetition of the other, subject to certain operations of transformation. Hence the concept of paranoia is not isolated but exists in series with an earlier concept, namely, that of monomania. The same applies to the concept of IQ in relation to that of imbecility, and so on. These terms are not synonymous, they are not the "same" concept, but one still "recognizes" the concept because its unity, the way in which it is distinguished from other concepts, remains more or less stable. Thus Foucault writes that we can trace "certain present-day notions back to Esquirol, Heinroth, or Pinel . . . whereas if we try to trace the development of psychopathology beyond the nineteenth century, we soon lose our way, the path becomes confused, and the projection of Du Laurens or even Van Swieten on the pathology of Kraepelin or Bleuler provides no more than chance coincidences."[43] The word "projection" does indeed indicate that the terms are defined by their relationships with other, neighboring terms. Thus we can conceive of a circle in an oval because the relationships of proximity and distance between the points remain stable, even if the identity of the points is not the same (some overlap with others and so on). Similarly, we can establish a series of concepts where the relations of proximity and distance between the concepts are not so disturbed that we can no longer be sure that we are dealing with the same divisions.

But these series don't matter either individually or even in their continuity. What is most important is the fact that they reveal gaps, discontinuities, and breaks. There is nothing more than homonymy between the word "madness" as it appears in Erasmus and then in Pinel. These words do not belong to the same series, and a conceptual space can't be projected between them. Of course, we need these homonyms to establish these serial gaps. It's because we believe that we are dealing with the same reworked and redefined term that we can establish that it actually occupies a completely different position in the vicinity of other terms where it's located. So it's not the "same" term, even with a different meaning. The Foucauldian method works in our areas of equivocality. People were locked up before the "birth of the prison"; so we believe that this was the same as what we mean by "prison," and that a history of the prison is simply an account of the transformations undergone by this thing or technique (or indeed, more broadly, the forms taken by the timeless imperative of punishment).[44] But if we stick to the serial method, we can see that it's not so much something that transforms across time, as a set of discontinuities that make up what we mean by "prison." It's a term that we project onto the past, at the cost of a fundamental misunderstanding, and that makes the very notion of punishment contingent when we restore the term in all its conditions. The goal of archaeology is to correct such misunderstandings using the serial method.

But the coincidence between several shifts of this kind is even more significant. Just as we can no longer prolong the monomania-paranoia series, we can no longer follow the imbecility-IQ series, or chronic encephalitis-general paralysis, insanity without delirium-character neurosis. We can also establish a correlation between Pinel's confinement of the insane in the psychiatric hospital and the new nosology.[45] So there is something like a lateral fault line through these series, and this is the event that can be defined as the correlation between these discontinuities across several series—*and by nothing else*. There can be no attempt to find a fundamental cause beneath this lateral fault line. The event is not so much the transformation of a term as the covariation of a group of series. This group owes its unity only to all these variations: so the present prison is *characterized* by the system of its differences from the past. Each must be regarded as the strict variant of the other. This idea of the event simply amounts to considering it as a structural mutation. It means that the event is not so much something that happens to a particular term at a given point but rather a transformation of the relationships between terms. This system, however, is "nondeductive"[46] since no attempt is made to deduce these different shifts from one another, so as to bring them back to the unity of an Idea. This is something that Hegel does, for example, seeking to deduce all Roman law from the notion of subjective freedom, itself defined as a development of the contradiction implied in the idea of freedom. Instead, the idea is to define the system by the covariation of these shifts. It's in this sense that Foucault is able to say that systems have no "interiority" of their own.

Finally, Foucault shows that new terms and new series appear along one side of this fault line that don't appear at all on the other side. Here it's no longer just a matter of a displacement in the relationship of proximity between terms but of the appearance of terms that were previously completely absent in the area under consideration. Thus "crime" enters into a conceptual space next to "madness" under the name of "homicidal monomania."[47] It is then that you can see that it isn't a question of a closed combination but of the transformation of a space that makes new things possible. It's not that some terms have replaced others, but the very ground itself has changed. Certainly, "madness" and "crime" are ambiguous terms. But the event needs to be defined as much by shifts of series as by the mapping of our equivocalities.

So for an event to exist we need (1) a series of terms that are defined by their proximity to other terms in projectable spaces; (2) discontinuities within these series; (3) correlations between these discontinuities; and (4) the appearance of new terms within these proximities. The "death of man" Foucault speaks of in *The Order of Things* is an event in this sense.[48] It is nothing other than the fact that certain relationships between certain statements have come undone. It is a discontinuity that appears only through the correlations that can be observed between the gaps in three series: the economic series, the biological series, and the linguistic series. It is a system of shifts at the end of which we can see that the word "man" is nothing but an ambiguous term, a term that has lost the architectonic function it had in the previous system. The death of man is like that of God: it is one of those silent events that Nietzsche talks about. It is not something that happened to a being; rather it is this "being," man, which is only a surface effect of the displacement of the relationship of serial changes between small particles of language.

The Being of Power: Introduction to the Event—Concept Number 2

It might seem that the concept that we have just presented of the event as structural change boils down to conceiving of change precisely in the way we have said it shouldn't be, namely, as the passage from one state (a certain configuration of relationships between terms) to another. Instead of things and properties, we have terms and the relationships between these terms. But in both cases, there would be a succession of static realities. This is not the case. First, we must remember that there is nothing *underneath* change except equivocalities. For example, it's not really as though we have gone from one global configuration of the universe—from one immobile slice of all that exists—to another—as in the fiction of Laplace's demon—or from one image to another on a strip of film.[49] There is no strip of film, any more than there is a total Universe. Besides, as we have said before, each system is not only a recombination of elements (even if these are ambiguous) but the emergence of a new space. Hence we can say that there are changes, but not that *something* changes. But most important, the "systems" that Foucault talks about are not real unities: they can only exist through the set of transformations that put them in relation with each other. It is not about defining the event as the passage of one system to another, but rather of defining each system by all the deformations through which it tears itself away from its other. In *The Order of Things*, the identity of our contemporary context is nothing other than the "death of man," in the same way that the Classical age has an identity than which is separate from both the *episteme* of the Renaissance and that of the "modern" era of the human sciences. History cannot be defined as a succession of eras. Instead, each "era" is a mutation of others, which make up a kind of virtual orb determining each age by its difference, by the way in which it doesn't collapse into the others. Thus Foucauldian being is made up only of rifts, without there being anything to rupture. If we ought not to be looking for *causes* beneath these mutations, it's precisely because we need to define each system by the set of all the operations that need to be put into place to separate it from the others.

Deleuze emphasizes that Foucault's introduction of concepts linked to "power" had nothing to do with a desire to respond to criticisms of irrationalism after he had refused to explain change but is instead a radicalization of the Foucauldian move to "eventalize" his objects of study.[50] In fact, after that point, each entity was characterized not only by the system of its differences from others but also by all the effective operations through which it tears itself away and continues to tear itself away from the other virtual combinations which surround it. We know that for Foucault, what characterizes power is its instability. Power is not owned, it must be exercised. The power relationship is a relationship of one force to another by means of which one "makes someone do" something, but in such a way that the balance of power never stabilizes.[51] But as Deleuze remarks, basically if power needs to be exercised, it is precisely because every force has the capacity to interact with other forces. What Foucault calls a "diagram" would thus correspond to an attempt to capture power in its very instability, that is, at the point where the captured forces are always ready to be captured by others.[52] All force is stolen by one force from another force. The relation of forces would in fact be a relation of three terms:

the force that is exercised, the force on which it is exercised, and the force against which it is exercised. In practice, we need to outline a diagram in terms of this anticapture that seizes a force by separating it from the force that tries to seize it in turn. But it can't do this once and for all; it has to continue to do so as power is exercised. Thus power is that element through which we communicate immediately and constantly with other possible configurations of our being and with other combinations of forces. This amounts to defining each system by its pure mutability, by its being as a variant in immediate relationship with other variants, beyond time. The past is never past: it is the virtual set of alternative diagrams against which any given system is defined—and can thus be defined as *pure mutation*. So instead of a succession of states along the time line, we now have all kinds of signposts, efforts, and strategies, which span time and define each *event* through its way of subsuming others. It's a battle that takes place in a mobile eternity—an eternity that is not always identical to itself but is something that can be defined intrinsically as change.

One would not be wrong in saying, therefore, that there was a shift in both Foucault's practice of critical history and the metaphysical concept of the event it led to. After this, pure change would not be a structural mutation or a new distribution of unities but the recapture of forces. The difference between these two definitions, however, is not as enormous as it looks. It's still a question of defining change as a reconfiguration of relationships between things, not as a transformation of a state of things. Simply put, the nature of the "relationship" (and therefore of things) changes considerably. For the still "structuralist" Foucault of *The Archaeology of Knowledge*, relationships are relationships of proximity, whatever he might claim, that is, of coexistence. Terms are defined by mutual relations, but one term never affects the other. On the other hand, for the Foucault of volume I of *The History of Sexuality*, relationships are *actions*. Actions need to be defined not by the given existence of intentional agents (because then history would once again be the history of heroes) but as relations of hierarchical integration. A force is defined by the way it becomes *part* of the exercise of another force that "makes it do" something. Thus in the pastoral relationship, grazing is something that the sheep does, but it is the shepherd who makes it graze, in the same way that it is indeed my computer that puts letters on the screen, but I am the one doing the writing. The force that the sheep exerts on the meadow is integrated into the force the shepherd exercises in relation to both sheep and meadow, meaning that the sheep is in fact "grazing." If the shepherd wasn't there, the sheep would be doing something else in the meadow, and it wouldn't be a sheep. Of course, all these terms are defined by their reciprocal relations (there is no shepherd without a sheep either), but there is an asymmetry between the terms: the action of one integrates the action of the other. Besides, it's this relationship of hierarchical integration (which is not the same as a relationship of spatial integration) that Nietzsche defined as the will to power. But again, this hierarchical integration must be defined by the set of techniques it uses to fight against hierarchical disintegration. The possibility is always open that the integrated term might enter into a relationship of hierarchical integration with other terms—which can also be described as resistance. The integrator term also has a tendency to enter into relationship with other forces. Hence no element is entirely defined by its relationships of integration but can be considered ultimately as *any element whatsoever*, that is, a pure capacity to contract hierarchical relationships with others, relationships through which it can be defined. This is undoubtedly another and more radical conception of the event. The latter is no longer so much a nondeductive system of homologous disconnections from heterogeneous series as a *set of reversals of the hierarchical integration of any element whatsoever.* Whether this Deleuzian interpretation is accurate or not, following on from Foucault, we can see that we're not able to respond in all cases to the question of what happened by seeking to establish the facts, and the transformations of these facts as they follow on from each other. We should instead respond by looking for what we are, specifically, as a pure passage, a fleeting flash where the kaleidoscope of history makes a sharp turn, and at the end of which we can no longer recognize ourselves in any particular objective condition. We then blend into that breach in time where we are located. A breach from where all kinds of sometimes familiar and sometimes disturbing masks bubble up, which look nothing like us but form everything we know about ourselves.

CINEMA'S EFFECT ON THE METAPHYSICS OF THE EVENT

After reconstructing the Foucauldian ontology of the event in this way, why turn to cinema? Haven't we answered the question we have set ourselves adequately? How can we expect to find in a few films a better way of developing this concept of a becoming that escapes history, and its categories of succession, accidents, substance, transformation, and so on? Let's begin by making the observation that the question remains *open.* The fact that Foucault was able to change the answers he gave, the fact that in his turn, Deleuze was able not only to attempt to reconstruct the response of his friend for his own benefit but also to propose an alternative response proves that we are not dealing with a definitive doctrine here but with an open problem, a work in progress. We are dealing with the task of extracting the concept of a nonhistorical becoming, of an insubstantial event and nonchronological change from concrete critical practices. Even if film has approached this problem on its own terms, there's no reason not to try to evaluate the metaphysical effects of its inventions in the same way. Just as Foucault's ontology of the event can't be separated from his critical practice of history, so we might hope to find in the way film separates the past from its historical interpretation a way of imposing a diagnosis of the transformation of our fundamental metaphysical categories that is just as powerful as the one we needed to account for the effect of Foucault's work on the ontology of the event. Of course, the fact that Foucault was a philosopher helps us to develop this question better, since he himself conceptualized his own process, but Foucault approached this question mainly through his practice of history and through his use of the past. Film can be just as much a way of relating to the past in terms of extracting pure becomings.

That film has come across this problem of a nonmemorial relationship to the past at various points in its history is not in question. Its history is certainly divided by different uses of history. Very early on, almost from the outset, it was pressed into service rewriting the past. And very early also, it was divided over this issue: one has only to think of the debate between Eisenstein with Griffith.[53] And we know that film initially set itself up as the art of events, the art that would accurately capture becoming outside of time. It was Dziga Vertov's grand project to use the camera to show the truth of the world using fragments of this very world—and this truth for Vertov, as for Foucault, is pure movement: "We affirm the kino-eye, discovering within the chaos of movement the result of the

kino-eye's own movement."[54] It is about clarifying the chronological processes of transformation, the pure event, what actually *happens*—for example, *today* as an event: "A day of visual
impressions has passed. How is one to construct the impressions of the day into an effective whole, a visual study?"[55] Vertov
has no hesitation in comparing this work of *investigation* to that
of the political police, the GPU: "To separate out and to bring
to light a particular issue, a particular affair."[56] Foucault could
have made this phrase his own—on condition that it was precisely the curiosity of the GPU and the "problem" that preoccupied it that needed to be clarified. According to Vertov, we
know that film has this capacity to extract pure becoming from
the processes of the world through montage. It's not enough to
record things as they happen: the truth of movement is not in
the sequence of transformations of objects but in the reorgani-
zation of movements. He provides a very simple illustration
that contrasts the overall image you have of a boxing match or a
dance spectacle from your seat in the theater to the internal
analysis that the camera can make of the event, not as the overall action of a body on a body but as a sequence of movements:
"A system of successive movements requires the filming of danc-
ers or boxers in the order of their actions, one after another . . .
by forceful transfer of the viewer's eye to the successive details
that must be seen. The camera 'carries' the film viewer's eyes
from arms to legs, from legs to the eyes and so on, in the most
advantageous sequence, and organizes the details into an
orderly montage study."[57] Unlike Foucault, Vertov doesn't need
to define the event by its external difference with what it could
have been. He is looking for what is *within* the situation that
will allow us to extract the pure event, the "problem," "the
case," in short, what is really happening. He is already dealing
with movements. But Vertov notes that these movements don't

somehow exist prior to editing but exist through what he calls "intervals," that is, cuts that link one movement to another, each making up a "shot."[58] Movement is not what happens in a shot but what happens from one shot to another. Every shot reciprocally qualifies the other during this passage: this is the full meaning of the famous Kuleshov effect. The essence of movement is to spread and to merge into another movement. This is why film can be the operator of a real metaphysical reversal. Things don't come before events that are the actions or passions of these things; instead it is events that come first, determining things and their accidents as media for an event that is never reducible to these things. It's not a train that arrives at the station but the arrival at the station as it is actualized by a section of train.

Deleuze, in his two great books on cinema, took this kind of claim seriously and tried to draw out all the philosophical consequences of the argument that film is the art of extracting pure becoming from the states of things.[59] But our problem is more limited. We need to know first how film goes about undoing history, transforming our relationship to the past by separating it from the identificatory uses we ordinarily make of it, making memory the instrument not of a grand recollection of objective facts but rather of an eventalization of the present, in short, knowing how film functions as a *critique* in Foucault's sense. Next, we need to examine whether we can extract a concept of the event or becoming from the concrete operations through which it produces its effects. Therefore we should include only films that adopt a position in relation to the past and a critical relation to that past—films that have done what Foucault did in the field of history. We will limit ourselves to two examples here so that we can provide a sufficiently detailed idea of the method and its effects.

I, Spectator of *I, Pierre Rivière*: The Event—Concept Number 3

One film immediately springs to mind: René Allio's, *I, Pierre Rivière* (1976). This film resulted directly from the interview with Daney, Bonitzer, and Toubiana that was our starting point.[60] Indeed, the editors of the *Cahiers* contrasted *Lacombe, Lucien* not to another film but to the book edited by Foucault as a model of another relationship to the past and to the memory of popular struggles, and as a model of an alternative way of talking about these struggles without speaking on behalf of those who were engaged in them.[61] Allio's work, as was already evident in *The French Calvinists* (1972) and *Rude journée pour la reine* (1973), was closely informed by the idea of a nonideological militant cinema, a cinema that would contribute to "giving history back to the people," a history not of grand events but of the micro dramas that form the fabric of day-to-day life: "Giving history back to the people. This is all I tried to do in my films. But history is also the times of crisis, the debates, the revolutions and the obscene struggles of my characters embedded up to their necks in the glue of the everyday. These are their 'historical moments.'"[62] So Allio would appear to be testing the *Cahiers* hypothesis, undertaking a "comparison" that was not "unproductive" between a book and film, turning an "adaptation" of Foucault's book into the protocol for an experiment that could measure the effectiveness of this meeting between film and philosophy on the terrain of a nonhistorical relation to the past.

It might seem that this was a somewhat literal manner of taking up the suggestion of turning the book into a film. But this was because Allio had understood that there was a process as general as Brechtian distantiation in the book's procedure and in Foucault's overall approach. This approach involved keeping with what was said in the way it was laid out and not seeking to interpret it, explain it, or even unify it. In other words, it was a new way of thinking about "ideological struggle" in general, in a manner not limited to one medium in particular. This process allowed for the presentation of a truth about the experience, removing it from the ideological scenarios that muzzled it in advance, but without replicating the effect of domination that structured the very act of speaking (telling the truth about what was silent): "giving a voice" to those without a voice but without "speaking for them."[63] Thus Allio was not seeking to "adapt" *the story*, that is, to transfer the written traces of the event (a young peasant kills his mother, his sister, and brother) to film, even if it was from that peasant Pierre Rivière's "point of view." To do so would have meant the loss of what was interesting about the book, specifically the fact that it was content to simply stage the conflict of discourses around the event. It was as if the event could only be grasped through the impossibility it created for language to say anything unique about it, to be able to sum it up with a definitive qualification—"this was an act of cruelty," "this was an act of madness," "this was an act of rebellion," and so on. Rivière's memoir has meaning only in the way it forms a balance of power with other discourses around it. Allio understood very well that it was in this conflict, in this "battle," that the event itself resided.

But while the book can only recapture this battle through the dispersion of words, film can add something else, namely, the conflict between words and bodies. Allio decided early on to stick strictly to the archive (almost every sentence in the film is in the book), and also to choose nonprofessional actors, actors who were peasants, admittedly not from the actual village where Pierre Rivière lived (and killed) but from a few kilometers away. This was not to provide more "realism" and to better reconstruct the event in his film. Instead, the aim was to show how the archive works through bodies, and how the word enters the flesh through concrete operations, enforcements, violence, and negotiations. It's about lending to language the crackles, the pops, the tiny resistances and sometimes marvelous tricks that produce the effect of meaning and making these heard through the illusory transparency of the world—a world in which sentences appear to simply unearth a truth already buried in things. It is this molecular battle where actions cannot be reduced to words and where sentences mold bodies, which was and continues to be the true subject of the film: not the epic of the Word made Flesh, but the battle without armistice of the archive that is written in and on the body.

Foucault was of course particularly sensitive to this aspect of Allio's film:

> I don't think that the film claims to be true. The film doesn't say that this is Pierre Rivière. What's historically convincing about Allio's enterprise is not that it's reconstructing the Rivière case. The film took the documents, the memoir, what was actually said by someone named Pierre Rivière, what was said by his family, by neighbors, by the judges, and asked how these words, these questions, these gestures might be put into the mouths, bodies, and attitudes of present-day people. These people were not even professional actors but peasants from the same locality, isomorphic to those involved in the 1836 case. This allows us to revive the question in a location as close as possible to the place where it was originally raised.[64]

This is a problem that is in fact very close to the problem that lies behind the "Lives of Infamous Men" project. It's about dealing with the event, not only in terms of the shift of relations between statements but also as a force that expresses itself through the language that had to be deployed in order to erase it, thus making apparent the changeability of the situation and its inherent instability as in all balances of power. But in particular, we can see even more profoundly here the problem that emerged in the fine text on Magritte.[65] It is perhaps in this latter text that Foucault provides his most precise instruments for a rigorous description of the way film works. He carefully analyzes the different ways in which Magritte explored a whole set of mobile relationships between words and images, once the ideal synthesis of classical mimesis is undone that associates a scene in perspective and a *historia*. He actually describes these relationships as a "battle": "We must therefore admit between the figure and the text a whole series of intersections—or rather attacks launched by one against the other, arrows shot at the enemy target, enterprises of subversion and destruction, lance blows and wounds, a battle."[66] Like Magritte, Allio's approach to film breaks the stable relationship of designation between words and things but with different tools. He makes the screen the "nonplace" where the combat between language and image takes place, preventing language from taking a bird's-eye view of the subject matter and constituting it from a distance as an *object*. This also allows it to function as a *question* aimed specifically at those who are asking the questions and leading the investigation. In short, his film functions as a *critique of the present*. Only then can the question "who is Pierre Rivière?" be asked again as a question addressed to the present: who are you, you who is asking the question?

It is precisely because of this audiovisual dimension (archives and bodies) that film can address the problem Foucault posed in new ways and with singular effects. This dimension is admittedly not foreign to Foucault. Deleuze notes, of course, that Foucault's concept of knowledge is an audiovisual one. It's about knowing how to put two dimensions that have acquired their own autonomy back together. On the one hand, you have regimes of discourse that need to be analyzed on their own terms, without basing them on what they refer to. For example, the delinquent is first and foremost a concept that needs to be defined laterally by its relationships with other concepts. On the other hand, you have regimes of visibility, which also need to be analyzed on their own terms, for example, the creation of the clinic opens up a new gaze, as does the Panopticon.[67] But this can only be done in that strange space that Foucault speaks of in relation to Magritte, this "nonplace" where the relationships between what can be said and what is visible are not stable. Only then is a "history of truth" possible, because there is no ready-made form for the truth, or for the meeting of words and experiences. Instead, there are all sorts of complex negotiations that need to be reconstructed case by case. It is at this precise point that Deleuze grasps the decisive function of film in Foucault's understanding of the event: "The archive, the audiovisual is disjunctive. So it is not surprising that the most complete examples of the disjunction between seeing and speaking are to be found in the cinema. In Straub and Huillet, in Syberberg, in Marguerite Duras, the voices emerge, on the one hand, like a 'story/history' [*histoire*] without a place, while the visible element, on the other hand, presents an empty place without a story/history."[68] The systematic use of these disjunctions between sound and image is undoubtedly one of the characteristics of "modern" cinema as studied by Deleuze in *The Time-Image*.[69] We see this in Bresson, in Resnais, in Godard, and in the Rossellini of *The Taking of Power by Louis XIV* (1966).[70]

But unlike Godard, Straub and Huillet, Duras, and many others, Allio doesn't adopt so much a particular process as a very detailed and very precise exploration of the different relationships that can be established between sound and image, as Deleuze himself remarks in a note.[71] This is how he manages to avoid reconstructing a history, re-creating its own unique element of instability and nonheroic conflict. This starts from the most complete disjunction, such as that which accompanies the opening credits of the film with the image of a field through a fence over which is heard the clamor of a court—showing a maximal distance between land marked by ownership and labor and the discourse of the state—and goes to its most classical manifestation in the dialogues where speech comes from the bodies we see. Between the two extremes, we see all sorts of subtle captures of image by sound and sound by image, which could be comprehensively cataloged, beginning with a very specific use of the relationship between the voice-over (speech detached from the body) and the voice on the screen (speech coming from the body) in different sequences.

As we don't have the space to highlight the systematic character of this exploration in Allio's film, we will provide just a few examples. One of the most spectacular is probably the scene of Pierre Rivière's first cross-examination in the office of examining magistrate, which shows the grave and silent face of the law, while a voice declares: "I, judge Exupère Legrain etc." One is tempted to think that this is a voice-over telling us in the past tense about a scene that we are seeing in a distant present (as was the case in the immediately preceding sequence of Pierre Rivière's arrest). But this impression is quickly contradicted by the tracking shot gliding across the face of the clerk reading the text we are hearing, and we understand that it has been dictated by the judge we've just seen. A mouth that says "I" in the present without having to move—can a more precise picture of the law be given than this? This image has all the more impact in that it follows directly on from a dialogue specifically with the accused, a dialogue that is also a veritable struggle between the investigator and the investigated, and at the end of which Rivière decides to speak and effectively explain himself.

Prior to this scene, the film has already set up subtle disconnections between the image and the word. It begins with a long silent shot of the corpses, which the camera scans from end to end, without ever giving us an overview. So we have simple bodies to begin with, bodies that can no longer speak—and then, off-camera, a voice, a cry (which we later identify as being the grandmother's): "Oh my God what a tragedy! Oh my God, what a tragedy!" This is then followed by the image of a young woman appearing in the doorway. Here, body and speech are reconciled in one simple statement: "They're all dead." A cry, the most basic form of verbal reaction, then a statement, the most basic form of commentary.[72] On the other hand, the initial findings are presented in voice-over. The doctors and the court clerk set themselves up silently among the corpses. Allio takes great care to show what action in relation to things is needed in order for discourse about them to begin. For instance, he shows how the representatives of medicine and law (whose responsibility it is to make things talk) step over the corpses, the way in which the clerk must sweep aside the objects of everyday life on the table in order to begin his work, his unease at being literally at the foot of a corpse. There is a whole cumbersomeness of things that the material apparatus to make them talk must arrange itself around and find a space. Pen and paper are the first instruments, things among other things, like the bowls and cauldrons, the sewing materials and the wooden clogs, the handwriting and the foot of the dead woman. Then speech begins: a man writes and we hear in voice-over what he is writing. It is thus the act of writing that allows the first transition to voice-over, while at the same time conserving a certain contemporaneity of text and image.

The next disconnection of word and image takes place during the first statement with the prosecutor arriving at the scene to carry out the first cross-examinations. The scene starts with dialogue, where the notables introduce and congratulate themselves. These dialogues are among the few (and very short) verbal sequences added by Allio. The scene continues with the prosecutor questioning Rivière's father. But the father's response is quickly covered by an external voice-over with a different accent—and what is accent if not the trace of the body in language? In this way, we witness how disembodied truth appropriates the facts, covering up the way those who actually went through them speak about them. The monument-voice, the voice of history that says what took place, replaces the witness-voice and speaks, or rather writes, in its place. The scene involving the physical and moral description of Pierre Rivière is even more impressive as it uses the process we analyzed in the confrontation of Pierre Rivière with the examining magistrate for the first time. We see the image of the family in front of the coffins, plunged into silence as the only adequate response to death and "tragedy." At the same time we hear someone reading the public prosecutor's physical and moral description of the suspect, relying on information that claims to be objective. It is objective to the extent that it offers an almost biometrical description and also because it purports to summarize the testimony of the very people who are silent. It concludes that the subject was a monster of cruelty recognized as such from childhood. A camera movement then shows the public prosecutor dictating these words to his clerk *beside* the grieving family, as if the voice of official truth comes not only to artificially cover up the voices of the witnesses but to occupy their silence. They are doubly mute, doubly defeated, first by "tragedy" and then by "justice." At the opposite end of the spectrum is Rivière's adoption of a voice in the writing of his memoir. A shot of the paper on which he writes his first words is cut, then Rivière stands, facing the camera, the same man who spoke only obliquely to the authorities, and enounces his text as he wrote it: "I, Pierre Rivière, having slaughtered my mother, my sister and my brother. . . ." It is no longer texts that cover up voices but rather the voice that takes the place of the text in a perfect substitution of hand and mouth: a mouth that says "I" for the first time with his body, but it is to say, alas! "I have slaughtered."

Many other shots could be analyzed showing how rigorously Allio explores this intertwining of voice and body, speech and images. We will limit ourselves to noting that these complex interplays are based on the existence of a mixed entity, that thing-word, that picture-voice which is *writing*. The end credits reverse the opening credits with precision, showing the same field divided by a fence and on either side a man and a woman, each carrying a sheet of paper in their hands, probably the property rights, but invisible to the viewer, thus unreadable. The sheet of writing is both the operator of the conflict between humans as well as the place of exchange between the visible and the sayable. The text introduces the paradox of a silent discourse, the possibility of both speaking and remaining silent. In this, it can only compete with one other surface, namely, that of the gaze. Speaking and remaining silent is also the province of the gaze. The grandmother's gaze appears in two very impressive shots: one that leads almost immediately into a quasi-Straubian panoramic shot of a landscape while a newspaper article is being read—the voice of rumor. The second shot is her response to the prosecutor who asks her, "And how was he with you Madam?" She just looks down pensively, as if she was *looking at the tragedy*, as if tragedy and misfortune was something you couldn't say or show, but which could only be thought. And it is this that Allio tries to do. *I, Pierre Rivière* is a wonderful film about tragedy and misfortune.

We can see here that in using a specifically cinematographic resource, an audiovisual resource, Allio manages to make of the past not a fact to be reconstructed but a question to be addressed to the very forms that are used to represent the past to the present. Film is perhaps one of the first audiovisual arts in our history, if we understand by this not so much producing sound and image at the same time (theater, opera, even dance do as much of course) but rather breaking the perceptual synthesis that forms our ordinary reality ("this is not a pipe"). Sound and visual elements are isolated and a whole interplay of coincidences and reattachments are implemented between these elements taking us to the heart, as it were, of the machinery of truth. Here, words and things are not simply passively existing things but energies, captures, and actions. They are images reaching out to series of words that interpret them, or conversely, words projecting a whole series of images that illustrate them, with neither being guaranteed to complement the other. But we can see also that basically, film does all this with the aid of a resource that is unique to it, namely, that of *mobile framing*; in other words, with the aid of this capacity to separate the source of the sound from the image that is in frame. As the fine shot of Pierre Rivière's first cross-examination shows, this process can shatter the most obvious unities that we believe allow us to capture events (complete sentences and individual organisms). We then descend into a complete molecular turbulence, where we find fragments of images and slices of language coming together in an unstable way: a silent face, a solemn self-presentation, a hand writing, a mouth reading, bloodstained objects, a sidelong glance, and so on. Or clogs lying on the ground, an overturned loom, a slit throat, a cry. Or again, two women arguing, a window closing, an old man's hand on a plane, a child's gaze.

This is the second aspect of Allio's film that made an impact on Foucault. The disjunction of body and language has the effect of preventing us from seeing bodies as the well-established agents of reasoned action under the full jurisdiction of discourse, of a legend, in the double sense of heroic narrative and that which tells us how to read an image. Rather, we see them as precarious media with boundaries that are always negotiable, surfaces of inscription and of composition for small, imprecise actions, for tiny movements that are no longer integrated into the body or incorporated into its matrix but detached from it completely. We see movements that travel across the body like so many relays, flowing from one to another, no longer actions of a previously formed organic body but acts without a subject whose composition creates a body on which these movements only seem to be hung as though pinned or suspended. "Our historical unconscious is made up of these millions, billions of small events which little by little, like drops of rain, erode our bodies, our way of thinking," wrote Foucault about Allio.[73] He rightly points out that Allio's interest in the everyday is not so much motivated by an interest in historical reconstruction as an interest in a kind of eternity made up uniquely of movements, passages, transitions, of those actions that mark the body rather than those actions the body performs, and which seem endowed with a life of their own. "It's the eternal present of what is most fleeting, that is, the everyday" that makes these "micro events that don't merit a mention and which more or less disappear from memory" but which are "still in some way inscribed in the bodies of twentieth century urban inhabitants."[74] Behind the sudden drama and the explosion of violence, there is the continuous hum of small, everyday squabbles, all these infinitesimal divisions that law and civil regulations organize and that mark the body of the earth and humans. Rather than an extraordinary act, we have "intensities, rumblings, things that aren't quite heard, layers, repetitions, things that are barely said."[75] Another way of reading the archive is through the bodies of the Norman peasants. It's those accents, those oblique head movements, those meditative glances, that way of lifting furniture or walking, in short, those bodily techniques that film has the unique capacity to detach from the body, making their transhistorical nomadism felt in their own specific autonomy.

In film, you don't see a woman walking but a woman's gait, a gait detached from the body where these movements are actualized and captured in this state, in this "phase" (in the sense of indicating a solid, liquid, or gaseous state), where it can jump from one body to another, a little like the vocal intonations that allow one to identify a friend, a relation, a teacher, in the body of another. It's probably worth mentioning that Marcel Mauss made the same remark specifically in the introduction to his famous article on "The Techniques of the Body." Mauss said he owed this concept, which was to become immensely popular in the sociological literature, to film: "A kind of revelation came to me in hospital. I was ill in New York. I wondered where previously I had seen girls walking as my nurses walked. I had the time to think about it. At last I realised that it was at the cinema. Returning to France, I noticed how common this gait was, especially in Paris; the girls were French and they too were walking in this way. In fact, American walking fashions had begun to arrive over here, thanks to the cinema. This was an idea I could generalise."[76] Thus film shows not tensed hands but the tensions arising among other forces, not eyes staring at something but gazes fixing on a face, not pruning hooks cutting throats but throats cut across time.

Foucault was always sensitive to film's capacity in this respect; indeed, all things considered, it was the only thing that seems to have interested him in film: this capacity to show bodies by removing them from their usual meaning and signifying function, molecularizing them at a level below the grand narrative integrations of the whole organism. This is what he found in Duras. So in relation to Lonsdale he notes "his gestures which are not attached to anything, which come through the screen towards you," and more generally about Duras's films, he comments on this "fog," this "mist," this "floating," where there are no things but only "emergences," "emergences without presence. You see the emergence of a gesture, the emergence of an eye: a character who comes out of the fog." It's as if Duras's films had the power to remove all solidity from bodies, offering them to us only in their original scattered form, as if they were made only of unstable equilibria, precarious unions between actions detached from any agent, gestures without a medium. We don't have mouths that speak but "voices without bodies," as Cixous says. We don't have people who observe the world and others but gazes that are "cut short," we don't have an actor who moves in three-dimensional space but "rumblings coming from who knows where," as Foucault describes them.[77]

Here, of course, we recognize those qualities without substance that Deleuze theorized in *Difference and Repetition*, whose model was Lewis Carroll's "smile without a cat."[78] Film does indeed grant us access to that Plimsoll line just below those large, deceptively natural unities, the bodies that form the basis for the moral and legal personality. Thus we can witness this teeming, this swarming, this rustling, where there are

no more than the larvae of gestures, the beginnings of movement, the imminences of the event, the lightest of touches rather
than contact, a whole inchoate and suspended world, perpetually in the process of creation. But better, we understand that
film is the art of extracting events from the substances in which
they are embodied, and to which we wrongly reduce them when
we think of events only as the decomposition of things. Film
has the capacity to put us into this universe without depth, into
this "formless fog" that Foucault compares to Bacon's or Blanchot's space and that he also qualifies as a "third dimension."[79]
One can't help thinking of that "great murmur of anonymous
discourses"[80] that appears as an object in *The Archaeology of
Knowledge* once the unities of the author, the book, and disciplines are dissipated, or of the "roar of battle" that concludes
Discipline and Punish.[81] We know that in this latter book Foucault attempts to analyze the body, not as an already established
unity and natural base for the moral and legal "personality" but
as a surface that is always slippery, which forms as a unity only
according to the conditions of a certain rule of the composition
of gestures, gazes, voices, and actions.

It's this same capacity to dissolve bodies and liberate their
"parts" from an organic unity that Foucault admires in Schroeter.
As he says in the interview on Sade:

> It is more a reduction, a granulation of the body, a kind of auton-
> omous exaltation of its smallest parts, of the minutest potentials
> of a fragment of the body. The body becomes anarchic, and hier-
> archies, localisations and designations, organicity, if you like, all
> come undone. . . . There is both a calculated and unpredictable
> encounter between the body and the camera, revealing some-
> thing, making an angle appear, a volume, a curve following a

track, a line, perhaps a wrinkle. And then, suddenly, the body is reconfigured, becomes a landscape, a caravan, a storm, a mountain of sand, and so on.[82]

Foucault stresses the fact that it is not about carving up parts of something and separating the organs from the organism (hence Schroeter's films are not "sadistic") but rather about freeing gestures and movements from their bases, letting them have value in their own right and returning them to their purely qualitative power. So we don't have something solid we can dig into but rather a surface where we can surrender to the delight of the very essence of sensation. What is displayed on the screen is not so much an image of the body, as bodies themselves reduced to their molecular state, pure movements, qualitative intensities, organized like vectors rather than integrated as parts. This is why Foucault sees film as the medium for what he calls "passion . . . a constantly mobile state, but it doesn't move to a given point."[83] These detached, purely qualitative movements are in fact pure intensities. They are always open imminences, suggestions, promises that are—in short, "becomings": a mouth that becomes a caravan, an insect's mandible, grassy crevices.[84]

One cannot help but think of Jean Epstein's wonderful words on *photogénie*:[85]

> A face is seen under a magnifying glass, exhibiting itself; it flaunts its fervent geography. . . .
> A theater of flesh.
> No vibration escapes me.
> Splendid warning for a mouth set to open.
> Compared to the drama of muscles moving in close-up, how paltry a theatrical performance made of words![86]

For Epstein too, what you see in cinema are pure *qualitative essences* in the exact sense in which Proust made them the object itself of art. "Film generalizes and determines. It's not about an evening, but *the* evening and yours is a part of it. . . . Instead of a mouth, *the* mouth, larva of kisses, the essence of touch."[87] Film has this strange power of distilling nonconceptual generalities that can be felt: not a smile but the *essence* of the smile, which is nonetheless not an abstraction, an idea, or a word but a sensation.

And for Epstein too, film can only distill the qualitative essences of the body on condition that it refrains from turning them into states in which things can be found (being red, being square, and so on.) Instead, it is about generating bodies as unending movements, imminences, deferments, suggestions, in short, pure becomings: "On the screen, the essential quality of a gesture is that it does not come to an end."[88] "The face which is getting ready to laugh is more beautiful than the laughter. One can stop there. I love the mouth that's about to speak, but which is still silent, the gesture which wavers between right and left, the step back before the jump, and the jump before it ends, the becoming, the hesitation, the coiled spring, the prelude and, better still, the piano being tuned before the overture. *Photogénie* is conjugated in the future and the imperative. It doesn't allow stasis."[89] Epstein offers a poetics of suspense and hesitation that is opposed to Vertov's view of the same effect. Becoming is not captured by infinite acceleration but through the extraction of the full particulars of a movement from its setting: "There are no stories. There never were any stories. There are only meaningless situations with no beginning, no middle, and no end and no right way up or down. One can look at them from any angle; right becomes left and without the limits of past and future, there is only the present."[90]

Finally, for Epstein as for Foucault, these qualities that are always becoming are emotional intensities, which snatch affect away from psychology, preventing its reduction to the emotional state of someone caught up in a drama, seeking to allow it to ignite with the greatest intensity on its own terms. "In cinema, sentimentality is impossible. Impossible because of extreme close-ups and of photographic precision. What is the point of having platonic flowers when the audience is looking at a face illuminated by forty arc lamps?"[91] Because it is an art of immediacy, film has the capacity to saturate everything that it shows with drama. The object is no longer just a thing that you see: it is caught up in premonitions, tensions and irruptions. "The real tragedy is in suspense. It looms over all the faces: it is in the curtain and in the door-latch. Each drop of ink can make it blossom at the tip of the pen. It dissolves itself in the glass of water. At every moment, the entire room is saturated with the drama. The cigar burns on the lip of the ashtray like a threat. The dust of betrayal."[92] Film *dramatizes* bodies, or, more precisely, it extracts dramatic intensity from bodies, their "share of ultraviolet."[93] Affect is no longer something that is added as an interpretation by a subject in relating to the object but is a dimension of the object itself, reduced to its vibratile condition. Instead of the false naturalness of the union of an organic body and a personal subjectivity, we have complex encounters between embryonic movements and affective intensities.

Thus we find in Epstein those three properties that ultimately characterize those fragments into which the body dissolves, the substance of the "formless fog" that Foucault mentions. These are the properties of qualities without substance, beginnings without states, affects without a psychological subject. Qualitative, inchoate, and intense, such is the world of bodies as it is captured on film. Epstein's argument is not unique, and Foucault does no more than rediscover the utterances of the first film theorists. Of course, Rancière is right in remarking that the great utopian idea of these pioneers was to believe that film was necessarily all this in and of itself. History has adequately shown that this was not the case, and indeed only became the case under certain conditions. It was not enough to put a camera in front of a thing to extract the molecular foundation where one finds the pure "eventalization" of each situation, and nothing is better than film in fostering the return of psychology, narrative, and even epic history.[94] But this just comes down to saying that ultimately, it's from itself that the film draws these qualitative becomings. This is exactly what we are saying as we seek to build an idea of the event beginning quite specifically from the operations in film that produce such eventalizations as *effects*, and effects of art. The montage—because it must be called that—that Allio constructs in *I, Pierre Rivière* is such operation.

Allio is probably not as radical as Schroeter, Duras, Straub and Huillet, or Syberberg. But he shows wonderfully how the two dimensions of cinema, its audiovisual aspects and mobile framing, can conjoin to make an instrument that is able to extract pure becomings from our relationship with the past. It should be noted, however, that this montage itself rests on two quite distinct properties, which both depend on location. In relation to sound, this essentially means associating a point and a zone (like any wave). In relation to images, it's a matter of being a part of a set of other images, which, however, never form a closed totality. As Bazin says, the screen doesn't create a frame but rather a mask: there is always something outside the frame.[95] Each of the assembled elements therefore has an expansive property, either because, like sound, there is never a single point to which it is necessarily attached, or because, like the image, it's always open to different compositions.

To conclude, if we had to distill a concept of the event from Allio's practice of film, as we have done from the historical practice of Foucault, we would have to say that an event is not a fact inscribed in the calm succession of states of the world but rather the *unstable resolution of a set of reciprocal micro captures put in place by various qualitative, inchoate, intensive, and communicative elements which themselves belong to at least two heterogeneous but mutually conditioned arrangements.* This definition is abstract, certainly, but it is nonetheless directly informed by Allio's practice of film and can be understood in relation to this. The fact that this is an unstable resolution can be understood as soon as one recalls that it is about the relationship of forces. Saying this is about captures simply means that the image determines what is said as much as the word determines the image. We have already sufficiently explained that these operations are molecular and shown that they descend below the organic or phrasal unit. That these elements are communicative refers to the broadcasting of sound and the composition of the image. We have provided a few examples of how these elements are arranged, and it's obvious that they both belong to different series (the mouth is not the word, the foot of the dead woman is not a written sentence, and so on). They are in a reciprocal relationship in the sense that, without one, you can't maintain the arrangement between the elements of the other. Without words, we wouldn't know how to group together the closed mouth of the prosecutor, the clerk's hands, the weapons on the table, or Pierre Rivière's shifty eyes. Although this analysis is built around film, and one film in particular, it must be given its greatest conceptual extension, and one might hope perhaps that it could help to clarify, indeed orient, other critical practices, even that of history itself. Metaphysics can also assist in this process.

Night and Fog, a Film Opposing Memory: The Event— Concept Number 4

I would like to propose just one other "case," one that seems particularly instructive. This case shows that the issue of a non-memorial relation to the past, aiming to wrest pure becomings from history with the present itself being eventalized, is not limited to the contexts in which Foucault conducted his own enquiries. We are speaking here of the classic historical documentary, Alain Resnais's film *Night and Fog* (1956).

Contrary, to what might initially be imagined, Resnais and Jean Cayrol's intention was explicitly directed against the idea of making a film of "commemoration." Resnais explains this very clearly in several passages of a remarkable interview about the film.[96] He wanted to avoid two pitfalls. The first was the kind of triumphal memory, which recalls past crimes so as to congratulate the present on defeating an enemy, thereby setting up a relationship of gratitude to the dead: the kind of recognition that can be seen in war memorials. As Resnais says:

> The most important idea for me was not making a "war memorial" film. I was really afraid of making a film that proclaimed "never again," "no this will never happen again," "it was all the wicked Germans' fault, but now that Hitler is dead, it's finished, it will no longer exist, and let's make every effort to ensure that it doesn't begin again." I felt that making a film like that was not the solution. So I really tried to push the film in the direction of

the question all this represents, namely the fact that something like this existed at the time, but when it comes down to it, other forms of the same thing have also occurred in the past.[97]

Resnais was equally opposed to the melancholy work of memory that refuses to let the past pander to the present by setting up a quasi-sacred relationship with the victims—sacred in the fairly strict sense that they should not to be subject to any instrumentalization. This is an attitude toward the past that is probably pretty much what ours is today, and which expresses outrage that we can make the dead serve any purpose, except the one of legitimizing the present that put a stop to the crime. The only worthy relationship we can have to the victims is to assume that their death had no meaning and cannot be "converted" into a positive history.[98] This implacably melancholy attitude toward the past probably found its highest philosophical and most poignant expression in Benjamin. But a more ordinary version is actually very common today. It's the simple statement that we owe something like a debt of pure memory to the victims. The right attitude toward such past crimes can be no more than infinite mourning, the inconsolable lamentation of the dead loss of so many human lives in the very absurdity of what is no longer really history—in short, silence.

Resnais had no words harsh enough to criticize what he describes as the attitude of "respect," which was also the argument invoked to ban his film at Cannes (these images could not be put in competition with others), or the concern about the possibility of commercializing these images: "Always respect." He explains very clearly that it's not a matter of replacing a triumphalist commemoration with a melancholy commemoration, but instead it's about making a film opposing memory: "There was this idea of questioning. That was it. I wanted a film that told people, not to 'remember'—which doesn't interest me—but to 'try and understand why this happens. And above all don't wait for it to happen before you start worrying about it.' I often spoke, as it were, of 'alarm bells': the terror that it would begin again. . . . It really was an enormous question mark, the whole thing of 'Who is responsible?' "[99]

So the film doesn't present a past that won't fade away in the register of the *unforgivable* but presents it in the register of *spectral contingency*. Here, the past is not a present state of affairs located on the continuous line of time at a different point from where we are now, but rather, it is a possibility that is still copresent with our own reality. This is what Resnais and Cayrol meant when they spoke of the *interrogative* character they wanted to give to their film. It was not about "not forgetting," or keeping the past in mind in a representation, but of posing a question about the present: "this could happen again, perhaps it is already happening again." This questioning of the present had first and foremost a political meaning for Resnais and Cayrol. It was about evoking the shadow of the camps in the colonial context.[100] But others saw the evocation of the camps in the Soviet context, which was also the reason for the Communists' initial unease about the film.[101] So this questioning partly addressed a given historical situation, a context, and an actual present. But it also had a metaphysical aspect, with the camps standing in as a revelation of a human possibility, a kind of essential general complicity with this crime, a doubt cast on ourselves and the very world where this was possible. It was a questioning that took place in relation to a spectral presence, a virtuality that was always there.

But there are two ways to understand this spectral "present" of the past. The first refers back to a theory of *nature*. If the crime is not merely a simple past we have left behind but something very close to us, then perhaps it refers to a nature: human nature according to a negative humanism, and it is this that Resnais has in mind, evoking something like chemistry.[102] Or perhaps it is something to do with the nature of power, along the lines discussed by Hannah Arendt, who calls into question the experience of obedience.[103] The problem with this approach to contingency is that it cannot answer the following question: yes, this is perhaps still possible, and we are certainly still capable of this, but why doesn't it happen all the time? The question is then displaced to the *context*, and it becomes a matter of "conditions" that are, or are not, "satisfied." Basically, this still creates just as much distance from the event, returning us to a current situation clearly indexed in time. We *could* certainly do it again if we were put in the same circumstances, but we could also take care to avoid such circumstances. The right question becomes not so much one of human nature or the nature of power but rather the question of the contexts that actually lead to the crime. But then the past once again becomes a present situation located at another point on the timeline.

The second response is more profound. It consists not in linking this "eternity of the past" to an ever present nature, but on the contrary linking it to a kind of radical contingency in our being. It consists in linking the past to the impossibility of being able to ensure the identity of the present, or of being able to circumscribe the boundaries of our condition, preventing us from being defined as variants of the being of torturers. Here, when we say, "we could have been Nazis," we are not saying "there are mechanisms in our natural constitution that are enough make us Nazis (if the right conditions are met)," but rather, "we can only define ourselves in relation to other forms of humanity, including Nazis." I communicate with other people not in identifying with them through a kind of lowest common denominator but rather through a whole host of transformations that situate me in my singularity in relation to others. They represent a possibility of myself, without my needing to separate things into an abstract nature, on the one hand, and a contextual particularity, on the other. It is simply because we take our places in relation to each other, forming together that strange crystal that is humanity. We are different facets of the same being defined only by the laws of the refraction of light from its facets. So here, we can see the past as a virtuality of ourselves: we are copresent with the past to the extent that we are differentiated from the past. Perhaps we need to say that according to the first interpretation, the past is only *possible*, whereas in the second it becomes truly *virtual*. It is no longer in the name of a nature but in the absence of a nature that we feel solidarity—or, more terribly, complicity—with other forms of humanity and life.

In short, the aim of this particular "historical film" is not so much to teach us something about the past but rather to make us, as spectators today, problematic in our own eyes. Who are we as we watch this film, as we enter into a relationship with these images? The effect is precisely about the *problematization* of the present, not about an understanding of the past.[104] The past serves here as a way of questioning the present about itself, of destabilizing the reassuring beliefs that the present might have about its own identity. So it is not from a point of view of confidence about ourselves that we relate to the past, but instead the past becomes a way of displacing ourselves and dealing with our own identity. This reversal, which consists in making of the past not something that should be observed but rather a point of view from which we must learn to see the present, is explicit in the final shots of the film where the collapsed ruin of the camp operates as a "strange observatory."[105] It's clear why this film can be seen as rigorously Foucauldian in its way of establishing a "relationship to the past."

This raises several questions. How does Resnais introduce into "historical film" the same questions and the same tensions that Foucault was able to introduce into the "history books"? And also, how can the comparison between these two formulations of the problem of a nonmemorial relation to the past, of a becoming counter to history, shed light on the metaphysical nature of the event, once torn from its spatiotemporal coordinates?

How does Resnais remove the past from history and memory? First, there is, of course, the tension he sets up between text and images. The text spells out the impossibility of transmitting this past into our present, therefore contradicting the archival images at the same time as they are shown. We are spontaneously tempted to assign these images the role of making us contemporary to the event, of putting ourselves in its presence. With the archival images no longer functioning as bridges thrown across the caesura of time, the film literally prevents us from *re-presenting* the past to ourselves (in the sense of making it present again), and thus of situating this event in our history in a very precise place that we can return to in imagination, measuring its distance in years or decades. Here, once again we can confirm the effectiveness of the disjunction between the word and the image—the failure to speak what we are seeing—in breaking the continuity of the past with the present, and in bringing forth a pure past.

Then there is the juxtaposition of archival footage and documentary footage, some in black and white, the rest in color, which as we know was at the time one of the most creative, but also one of the most expensive, decisions that Resnais imposed on his producers. But their difference is not a reassuring measure of the relationship between two states, the past and present, at the same time united and separated by the passage of time. Instead, they contaminate each other, swap functions, and bleed into each other. The documentary images confer on the archival images their status as mute ruins that cannot be made to speak, which will not give up their abominable secret. The archival images constantly threaten today's green, overgrown places with the possibility of a gray repetition of the crime. The color works paradoxically: instead of increasing the realism of the images, it condenses the inability of the image to communicate what it is speaking of: "we can only show you the shell, the color of this brick dormitory and this threatened sleep."[106] It's as if color separated us from things as time separates us from the past. The time difference thus comes to inhabit the image in the present and to split it wide open from the inside, as it were.

Finally, there are the tracking and panoramic shots that right from the beginning of the film show the spatial proximity between the space of ordinary life, which is also our present, and the unimaginable space, which doesn't quite recede into the past: "a peaceful landscape" (73). The disturbing proximity of present and past, their terrifying virtual copresence, is imposed through the unity of the shot, as if the past surrounded and threatened the present in the same way as what is out of frame holds in reserve other fusions of images that could entirely upset its identity. The present no longer appears to be linked to the past in the way that two images following on from each other do. Rather, the link occurs in the way two qualifications of what we see ("this is a meadow with flights of crows, crops, and grass fires") are reframed and fade abruptly into each other ("this is the site of a concentration camp") (73). If Resnais felt the need to film these ruined camps, instead of simply being content with archival footage, it's not so much to provide a visual testimony to the traces of the past crime in the present as to find a freedom of vision that archival images don't have. These archival images isolate scenes and separate spaces (the place where prisoners are assembled, the orphanage, the hospital, the domestic space of the commandant with his family and guests).

These three processes converge to show both the extreme distance and the extreme proximity of this event "which eludes those who were subjected to it" (87), preventing us from seeing the past in terms of an identity that is well-defined in time. It shatters the distribution of past and present and sets up between them what has to be called a becoming, namely, the always open possibility of one passing into the other.

Perhaps above all, what these three processes have in common is that each time, the present is separated from itself by that which it believes to be distinct from itself and to have banished to the exterior (the past, elsewhere). We detach from ourselves, we cannot quite identify with what we see, we cannot believe what we can see for ourselves, what we know. We are put in direct contact with the *unbelievable*. But this present that is formed through its own internal division, what is it but an *image*? *Night and Fog* exploits the most obvious but at the same time the most difficult resource in film, that is, its capacity to question that utterly singular ontological status of the image through which we are united with that which separates us from it. It keeps saying to us: "You are not seeing things but images, and images hide as much or even more than they show." The uneasiness that this gives rise to is not that film is incapable of communicating the extremity of what it shows, but rather that we are unable to grasp what happens to us because we insist on believing that our world is not made up of images. What do these very real ruins that we can visit and walk around in mean for us? "An image that is receding into the distance." What do these "peaceful surroundings" that open the film and in which

(here/there). It is because *the before* is *next to* that we find a kind of porosity between what we are and what we could be, and that we find ourselves directly (albeit virtually) in contact with other events on a surface of pure emergence.[107] Thus time ceases to be a vast enveloping framework where situations are distributed as quite distinct identities and instead becomes a fault line within everything, separating things from themselves at the same time as it puts them in an immediate virtual relation with everything else. It is no longer the past that belongs to our history but the present that becomes a part of a becoming, always artificially isolated, always precarious, never certain.

We can therefore say that there is a *becoming* when what is exterior to something also comes to divide it from within and prevents it from corresponding with itself. What happens to us in *Night and Fog* is that we can no longer quite merge into the present or completely identify with it. The film breaks the relationship we have with the present world and what is directly in front of us, leaving us with the feeling that we are not what there is, but rather we are the incompleteness of what there is. But this incompleteness is essential, and not contingent. We can't complete the picture we have of ourselves by widening the field of vision: there is no complete picture. *Night and Fog* establishes a proximity, not so much between two parts of a global space as between two incompatible spaces, between two fenced-off systems, both intended to be finite. On the one hand, there is the familiar, the ordinary, and the domestic; on the other, the extraordinary, the unthinkable, the intolerable. Neither can be integrated into the other, and it is for this reason that they become images for each other. The extraordinary harshness of those shots of Goethe's oak at Buchenwald, of the zoo, of the greenhouses of rare plants, which make these traces of the "time before" appear inside the camp as a mockery of themselves, as simulacra. Similarly, the words "orphanage," "invalids' block" and even "prison" seem to be homonyms of what we usually understand by these terms.[108] The camp is "virtually a real city," writes Cayrol, but only virtually. What *Night and Fog* shows us is the juxtaposition of two incompossible spaces, spaces that are incompatible with each other because they organize closed and alternative systems of possibilities. And yet they exist side by side. But they don't form an actual and verifiable whole that can be totally embraced and circumscribed. Their juxtaposition has the specific effect of preventing each actual state from closing in on itself and of splitting it to its core and in its essence, and allowing it to fall back down as a pure fragment, something incomplete, a contingency. This is the contingency of our present, which can always become the past, subject to a shift of vision, but also a contingency of the past that might not have been what it was. To say that the past and present exist side by side is to put the focus on the "freedom" Foucault spoke of himself in his wonderful text on critique.[109] There is a kind of optimism in *Night and Fog*.

If Foucault diagnosed becoming by establishing homologies between the shifts in heterogeneous series, Resnais does this by producing a series of *unframings* that, rather than integrating one image into another, glue together two incompatible worlds. Each becoming thus appears as a totality composed of two incompossible halves through which the outside continues to drive a wedge between us and ourselves. It is the spatial opening that comes to break the present apart and make time effervesce. We are separated from ourselves by the finite and open character of our situation. We have not so much a unified and complete picture as a *series of partial retotalizations that lead to continually intensifying fluctuations in the local totalities themselves*. So if we had to extract a concept of the event from Resnais's practice in this film, we could say that an event is *a whole divided within itself into two incompossible halves through a series of unframings and partial retotalizations that establish it as part of an always open whole.* We can describe these halves as *images* that are never able to form a closed totality but rather split it apart.

Again, in any case, it's clear that as with Magritte and Allio, a metaphysical reflection on the event informed by cinema leads us back to the question of space. We can grasp the eventality of our existence only if we stop considering space as a ready-made, self-evident, and self-assured given, framed by nature within a grand geometric framework that assigns us a place from where we can guarantee our ontological impenetrability. We can take hold of this eventality only by conceiving of space as a breach that is always ready to open, a precarious, and in some respects artificial construction, a sometimes disastrous protection against the outside. Indeed, we are not *in* space, we *are* that space— that "surface of emergence." Thus if cinema has a unique capacity to extract the event and its pure becoming from the present, it may be because it has this capacity to construct its own spaces, and instead of indexing the past in abstract chronological time, it can explore our relation to the past and use it to reconstruct that singular space that characterizes today.

We could continue our exploration by invoking many other cases, giving them just as much attention and taking the metaphysical suggestions they propose just as seriously. For example, the same kind of work could usefully be undertaken in relation to Éric Rohmer's *The Lady and the Duke* (2001), Gus van Sant's *Elephant* (2003), Quentin Tarantino's *Inglourious Basterds* (2009), or further, Claude Lanzmann's films.[110] We could also add Hans-Jürgen Syberberg's films (the most "vicious" of them all),[111] Peter Watkins, Jean-Marie Straub and Danièle Huillet, Luchino Visconti, Andrei Tarkovsky, the Roberto Rossellini of

The Taking of Power by Louis XIV (1966), and especially, of course, Jean-Luc Godard, the most intelligent of them all. Many more could be mentioned. In particular, we could show the way in which the introduction of digital techniques into film transforms the relation we can construct to the past and how the concept of the event reemerges profoundly changed. But we hope that these few pages, which are already too lengthy, can at least suggest the broad outline of a program that others might take up. We also hope that these pages are enough to show the fruitfulness of an approach that refuses, in what is, after all, a very Foucauldian way, to construct a metaphysics of events independently of the actual practices that give rise to this metaphysics, extracting it instead from the confrontation of these practices, whether verbal or not. In short, we hope that these few pages are enough to convince us to go to the movies with Foucault.

PART II

MICHEL FOUCAULT ON FILM

3

FILM, HISTORY, AND POPULAR MEMORY

C *ahiers du cinéma*: Let's start with the journalistic phenomenon that is the fashion for retro.[1] The question is basically: what makes films like *Lacombe, Lucien* (1974) or *The
Night Porter* (1973) possible today? Why do they provoke such
an enormous response? We think the answer to this should be
sought at three levels:

1. The political situation. Giscard d'Estaing has been elected.
A new kind of relationship to politics, history, and the political
system is coming into being, indicating very clearly and in a way
visible to all that Gaullism is dead. So, insofar as Gaullism
remains closely linked to the period of the Resistance, we need
to look at how this translates into film.

2. How bourgeois ideology might mount an attack
against orthodox Marxism (which is rigid, based on economics and mechanistic—the terms don't matter) and which
has for so long provided the only key for interpreting social
phenomena.

3. Finally, what this means for activists—given that activists
are both consumers and sometimes filmmakers themselves.

Marcel Ophüls's film *The Sorrow and the Pity* (1969) opened the floodgates. Something that had previously been either completely repressed or taboo has burst onto the scene. Why?

Michel Foucault: I think this comes from the fact that the history of the war and what took place has never really been recorded, other than in completely official histories. These official histories were essentially centered around Gaullism, which was both the only way to write that history in terms of an honorable nationalism, and also the only way of bringing in the Great Man as a historical figure and the man on the right, the man of old nineteenth-century nationalisms.

Finally, France was vindicated by de Gaulle, while the right—and we know how the right behaved during the war—was purified and sanctified by him. Consequently, the right and France were reconciled through this way of writing history. We must not forget that nationalism was the climate that produced the birth of history in the nineteenth century and also, in particular, the teaching of history.

What has never been described is what went on in the very heart of the country after 1936 and even what went on from the end of the 1914 war up until the Liberation.

Cahiers: So what has happened since *The Sorrow and the Pity* was made is a kind of return to truth in history. The question is whether it really is the truth.

Foucault: This needs to be linked to the fact that the end of Gaullism means a final end to the right's vindication by de Gaulle and by this overall period. The old Pétainist right, the old collaborationist Maurrasian and reactionary right, which camouflaged itself as best it could behind de Gaulle, thinks that it is now entitled to rewrite its own history. The old right, which was historically and politically discredited after Tardieu,[2] is now returning to center stage.

The right explicitly supported Giscard. It no longer needs to disguise itself and, as a consequence, can write its own history. And, among the factors that account for Giscard's current acceptance by half the French population (a majority of two hundred thousand), we shouldn't forget films like those we are discussing—whatever the intentions of the authors. The fact that they were able to be screened has allowed a certain form of consolidation on the right. Just as, conversely, the disappearance of the division between the national right and the collaborationist right has certainly made these films possible. These two factors are completely linked.

Cahiers: So this history is being rewritten in both film and television with debates such as those on *Dossiers de l'écran*[3]—which twice in two months has chosen the theme of the French during the Occupation. This rewriting of history is apparently also being undertaken by directors who are generally regarded as left wing. This is a problem that we need to examine in more depth.

Foucault: I don't think things are that simple. What I said earlier was very sketchy. Let's look at this again.

There's a real battle taking place. And what's at stake? It's what might broadly be called *popular memory*. It's absolutely true that people—and I mean those who don't have the right to write, produce their own books, or write their own history—these people still have a way of recording history, of remembering, of living it and using it. Up to a certain point, this popular history was even more alive and more clearly formulated in the nineteenth century, when there was, for example, a whole tradition of struggle that was transmitted orally or through texts and songs and so on.

A whole series of devices was put in place ("popular literature," cheap literature, but also school education) aimed at putting a stop to this movement of popular memory. One might add that this enterprise has been pretty successful. The historical knowledge that the working class has of itself is continually shrinking. For example, it's really quite remarkable when you think about what late nineteenth-century workers knew of their own history, and what the trade union tradition was like—in the strong sense of the term tradition—before the war in 1914. This has continued to diminish. It is diminishing but is not lost for all that.

Nowadays cheap literature is no longer enough. There are the much more effective means of television and film. And I think this is a way of *reencoding* popular memory, which still exists but is unable to find an expression. So people are shown not what they actually were but what they need to remember themselves as having been.

Since memory is, after all, a large factor in the struggle (it is, in fact, from within a kind of dynamic awareness of history that struggles develop), if you are in charge of the memory of the people, you are in charge of their vitality. And you are also in charge of their experience and their knowledge of previous struggles. And what the Resistance was must no longer be known.

So I think that we must understand these films along those lines. Basically, their theme is that there have been no popular struggles in the twentieth century. This assertion has been formulated successively in two ways. The first, immediately after the war, simply stated: "What a century of heroes the twentieth century has been! There was Churchill, de Gaulle, those chaps who were parachuted in, the squadrons, and so on!" This amounted to saying: "There was no popular struggle, the real struggle was this one." But no one has come out and said directly: "There was no popular struggle."

The other, more recent and more skeptical and cynical way of looking at things, if you like, consists in coming right out with the pure and simple assertion: "Look at what actually happened. Did you see any struggles? Where did you see people actually rising up and taking up arms?"

Cahiers: A sort of rumor, perhaps, has spread since *The Sorrow and the Pity*, namely, that the French people as a whole didn't resist. They even agreed to the collaboration and the Germans and swallowed it hook, line, and sinker. The question is, what does this all really mean? It does indeed seem that the issue at stake here is popular struggle, or rather the memory of that struggle.

Foucault: Exactly. It's essential to take possession of that memory, take control of it, govern it, tell it how it needs to function. And when you see these films, you learn what you need to remember: "Don't believe all you've been told. There were no heroes. And if there were no heroes then there was no struggle." This leads to a kind of ambiguity. The statement that "there were no heroes" is an active dismantlement of a whole mythology around war heroes of the Burt Lancaster school. It's a way of saying: "That's not what the war was about!" This creates an initial impression of stripping away history: we are finally going to be told why we are not obliged to identify with de Gaulle or the members of the Normandy-Niemen squadron and so on. But the sentence "there were no heroes" hides another, which is actually the real message, namely, "there was no struggle." That's what this is all about.

Cahiers: There is another phenomenon that explains why these films are doing well. It's because they use the resentment of those who actually fought against those who didn't fight. For example, people who were in the Resistance and who saw the passive citizens of a town in central France in *The Sorrow and the Pity* recognize this passivity. And from there resentment gains the upper hand, and they forget that they in fact fought.

Foucault: In my view, the politically important phenomenon lies in the phenomenon of the series rather than in any particular film. This is the network created by all these films and which, no pun intended, they occupy. In other words, what's important is the question: "Is it currently possible to make a *positive* film about the struggles of the Resistance?" Well, apparently not. You get the impression that people would laugh or quite simply, nobody would go and see the film.

I quite like *The Sorrow and the Pity*. I don't think that it was a bad thing to have made it. I may be wrong, but that's not important. The important thing is that this series of films correlates precisely with the impossibility—an impossibility emphasized by each of them—of making a film about the positive struggles that might have taken place in France during the war and the Resistance.

Cahiers: Yes. This is the first thing that's raised when we criticize a film like Malle's. The response is always, "What would you put in its place?" It's true that we don't have an answer to this. We should be starting to develop, as it were, a left-wing point of view on this, but it's true that a ready-made one doesn't exist.

The problem also reemerges of how to produce a new type of hero, a positive hero.

Foucault: The problem is not the hero but the struggle. Can a film be made about struggle without the traditional processes of heroization? We are coming back to an old problem here: how has history come to engage in the discourse that it has and to exploit what has happened, other than through the epic, and by offering itself as a story of heroes? That's how the history of the French Revolution has been written. Film has proceeded in the same fashion. This can always be contrasted with its ironic flip side: "No, look, there are no heroes. We're all swine, and so on."

Cahiers: Let's get back to the fashion for retro. The bourgeoisie has mainly focused its interest from its own standpoint on one historical period (the 1940s), which acts as a focal point for both its weakness and its strengths. This is where it is most easily exposed (it's the bourgeoisie who did the groundwork for Nazism and the collaboration), and it's also where it is now, in the most cynical way, trying to justify its historical attitude. The problem for us now is finding something positive in this same historical period. "Us" refers to the generation of May 1968 or LIP.[4] Is there a point of weakness in this period that we can use in one form or another to construct a possible ideological hegemony? It's true that the bourgeoisie is both on the offensive and defensive in relation to this subject (that is, its recent history). It is strategically defensive but tactically on the offensive, as it has found its strong point, a position from which it can better confuse the issue. As for us, should we simply be on the defensive and reestablish the truth about history? Is it possible to find that ideological weak point? Does that point automatically have to be the Resistance? Why not 1789 or 1968?

Foucault: Still on the same subject and thinking about these films, I wonder whether we might not perhaps come up with something else. When I say "subject," I don't mean either showing these struggles or showing that they didn't take place. What I mean is that it is historically true that when war was declared, there was a kind of rejection of war among the French masses. Now where did this come from? It came from a whole series of episodes that nobody talks about: neither the right because it wants to hide them, nor the left because it doesn't want to be associated with anything that might be contrary to the "national honor."

A good seven to eight million men went to war in 1914. They led a terrible existence for four years and saw millions upon millions of people die around them. And they ended up in 1920, with what? The political right in power, total economic exploitation, and, finally, an economic crisis and unemployment in 1932. How could these people, who were crammed into the trenches, still want war during those two decades from 1920 to 1930 and 1930 to 1940? For the Germans at least, defeat had revived in them a national sentiment such that the desire for revenge was able to overcome this kind of disgust. But at the end of the day, no one liked fighting those bourgeois wars, with those officers, for those kinds of benefits of war. I think this was a formative experience for the working class. When those guys dumped their bikes in the ditch in 1940 and said: "I'm going home," it's not a simple matter of saying "they were all spineless layabouts!" This is something that can no longer be hidden and needs to be situated within this whole sequence of events. The noncompliance with national guidelines needs to be given a place. What happened during the Resistance is the opposite of what we have been shown. Instead a process of repoliticization, remobilization, and an inclination for struggle gradually reappeared in the working class. It gradually reemerged after the rise of Nazism and the Spanish Civil War. But what these films show is just the opposite: that is, after the great dream of 1939 was shattered in 1940, people gave up. This process did indeed happen, but it took place as part of another, much longer process that was actually going in the opposite direction. This process, which began with distaste for war, culminated by the middle of the Occupation in the growing awareness that fighting was necessary. We need to ask where this idea—that there were no heroes only spineless layabouts—came from and where it's grounded. After all, have there actually ever been any films made about mutinies?

Cahiers: Yes. There was Kubrick's film *Paths of Glory* (1957), which is banned in France.[5]

Foucault: I think there was a positive political meaning in this failure to support calls for national armed struggles. You could look at the historical theme of the family in *Lacombe, Lucien*, tracing it back to Ypres and Douaumont.

Cahiers: This raises the problem of popular memory, which has its own specific temporality, quite removed from any institution of central power or the outbreak of particular wars.

Foucault: This has always been the goal of school history: teaching people that being killed is a sign of great heroism. Look at what has been made of Napoleon and the Napoleonic wars.

Cahiers: A certain number of films, including those of Malle and Cavani, abandon history and the notion of struggle in relation to Nazism and fascism and set up another idea in their place or on the sidelines, usually relating to sex. What's this about?

Foucault: Wouldn't you see *Lacombe, Lucien* and *The Night Porter* as being radically different on this front? It seems to me that the erotic and passionate aspects of *Lacombe, Lucien* have a function that is quite easy to spot. Basically, it is a way of making the antihero acceptable, of saying that he is not as anti as all that.

Effectively, all the power relations in his life are distorted and he makes them operate in a vacuum, but just as we expect his erotic relationships to follow suit, suddenly a true relationship emerges and he falls in love with the girl. On the one hand, there's the machinery of power that drags Lacombe along from a flat tire to something more and more insane. And on the other, there's the machinery of love that seems to be connected to this, and which also looks distorted. Instead, it works in the opposite direction and in the end restores Lucien to being a handsome, naked youth living in the fields with a girl.

So there's a kind of rather facile antithesis between power and love. In *The Night Porter*, however, the problem is a very important one—both in general and in the current context— it's the problem of the *love for power*.

Power has an erotic charge. This raises a historical problem: how is it that Nazism—which was represented by guys who were pathetic, second rate, puritanical, and the worst kind of Victorian spinster or at best perverts—how is it that now and everywhere, in France, Germany, the United States, in pornographic literature across the entire world, they have become the ultimate erotic point of reference? Every tinpot erotic fantasy now borrows from Nazism. When it comes down to it, this raises a serious problem: how do we love power? No one loves power anymore. That kind of affective erotic attachment, that desire for power, the kind of power that is exercised over you, doesn't exist anymore. Monarchy and its rituals were created to generate this kind of erotic relationship to power. The grand machinery of Stalinism and even Nazism was also created to this end. But it all fell into ruin, and it's clear that you can't love Brezhnev, Pompidou, or Nixon passionately. One could, at a pinch, love de Gaulle or Churchill or Kennedy. But what's happening at present? Are we starting to witness the re-eroticization of power, which we can see at one pathetic and pitiful extreme in the porn shops with Nazi insignia that one finds in the United States and also in Giscard d'Estaing's approach (a more acceptable but equally ridiculous version)? This approach involves saying: "We're going to parade down the streets in a suit shaking hands with people, and the kids will have half a day off." There's no doubt that Giscard has partly built his campaign not just around his imposing physical presence, but also around a certain eroticization of his persona and his elegance.

Cahiers: This is how he presents himself on an electoral poster, the one where you see his daughter turned toward him.

Foucault: That's right. He's looking at France, but she's looking at him. Seduction is being restored to power.

Cahiers: This is something that struck us during the election campaign, especially during the televised public debate between Mitterrand and Giscard. They weren't operating on the same terrain at all. Mitterrand came across as the old type of politician, belonging to the old left, let's say. He was trying to sell ideas, ideas that were a bit dated and old-fashioned, but he did this with great nobility. As for Giscard, he was selling the idea of power, exactly as an advertiser sells cheese.

Foucault: Again, until quite recently, you had to apologize for being in power. Power needed to be erased and not display itself as power. To a certain extent, this was how democratic republics operated. The problem was how to make power sufficiently insidious and invisible, so that what it was doing and where it was couldn't be pinned down.

Now—and here, de Gaulle played a very important role—power is no longer hidden, it's proud to exist and say: "Love me, because I am power."

Cahiers: Perhaps we could talk about a certain powerlessness in long-standing Marxist discourse in its failure to account for fascism. Let's put it this way: historically Marxism has accounted for the Nazi phenomenon in an economistic and deterministic way, completely leaving aside anything that might specifically relate to Nazi ideology. We might wonder, then, how someone like Malle, who is quite aware of what is happening on the left, can take advantage of this weakness and rush into the breach.

Foucault: The definition that Marxism offers of Nazism and fascism is as follows: "Overt terrorist dictatorship by the most reactionary fraction of the bourgeoisie." This is a definition that is quite lacking in substance and omits a whole series of links. In particular, it omits the fact that Nazism and fascism were possible only insofar as there was a relatively large section of the masses who took upon themselves responsibility for a certain number of state functions of repression, control, and policing. An important aspect of Nazism was its profound penetration inside the masses and also the fact that a part of the power was actually delegated to a certain fringe of the masses. This is where the word "dictatorship" is both true in general and false in particular. Let's consider the power that an individual could exercise under the Nazi regime simply by being in the SS or being registered with the party. You could effectively kill your neighbor and steal his wife and his house. This is where *Lacombe, Lucien* is interesting because it shows this side of things well. The fact is that, contrary to what is usually understood by dictatorship, that is, the power of one individual, you could say that this kind of regime gave the most dreadful, but in a sense the most intoxicating, part of power to a considerable number of people. The SS was the body that was given the power to kill and to rape.

Cahiers: This is where orthodox Marxism fails. Because this is what forces it to talk about desire.

Foucault: Desire and power.

Cahiers: This is also where films like *Lacombe, Lucien* and *The Night Porter* come into their own. They are able to talk about desire and power in a way that seems to be coherent.

Foucault: It's interesting to see in *The Night Porter* how the power of one was taken up and implemented by people under the Nazi regime. The kind of mock court that is set up is quite fascinating. It takes on the appearance of a psychotherapy group, but in fact it has the power structure of a secret society. Basically, it is a reconstituted SS cell, which is endowed with a judiciary power that is different and opposed to central government. You have to take into account the way power was distributed and delegated within the very heart of the population; and you must also take into account the tremendous displacement of power that the Nazis operated in a society like Germany. It's wrong to say that Nazism was the power of big business transmuted into another form. It wasn't the power of a beefed up top management. It was indeed all this, but only at a certain level.

Cahiers: This is indeed an interesting aspect of the film. But what seemed to us to be highly questionable was that it seemed to be saying: "If you're a classic SS officer, you operate in this way. But if you have a certain 'notion of expenditure'[6] as a bonus this makes for a wonderful erotic affair." The film therefore maintains the seduction.

Foucault: Yes, and it's here that it joins *Lacombe, Lucien*. Nazism never provided people with anything material; it never gave them anything other than power. You have to ask, if this regime was nothing other than a bloody dictatorship, why it was that on the third of May 1945, there were still Germans who were prepared to fight to the last drop of blood, if these people were not attached in some way to power? Of course, we must also take into account all the pressures and denunciations.

Cahiers: But if there were denunciations and pressure it's because there were people who were ready to denounce. So how did people get caught up in all of this? How had they been fooled by this redistribution of power of which they had been the beneficiaries?

Foucault: In both *Lacombe Lucien* and *The Night Porter*, the excess power they are given is converted into love. This is very clear at the end of *The Night Porter*, in which a kind of miniature concentration camp is set up around Max in the room where he is dying of hunger. So here, love has converted power, the excess of power, into the total absence of power. In a way, it's almost the same kind of reconciliation as in *Lacombe, Lucien*, where love turns the excess power in which he was trapped into a rustic destitution, a long way off from the seedy Gestapo hotel, also a long way off from the farm where the pigs were being slaughtered.

Cahiers: So we now have the beginnings of an explanation for the problem you were posing at the start of this interview: why is Nazism, which was a puritanical, repressive system, now universally eroticized? There has been a kind of shift. There's an avoidance of a central problem that no one wants to consider, namely, the problem of power. Or rather, this problem has been completely shunted into the sexual arena. So much so that this eroticization ultimately becomes a type of displacement or repression.

Foucault: This problem is really very difficult and perhaps hasn't been studied sufficiently, even by Reich. What makes power desirable and what makes it actually desired? The processes through which this eroticization is transmitted and strengthened and so on are clear. But for this eroticization to work, the attachment to power and the acceptance of power by those over whom it is exercised must already be erotic.

Cahiers: This is all the more difficult since the representation of power is rarely erotic. De Gaulle and Hitler were not particularly attractive.

Foucault: Yes, and I wonder if Marxist analyses are not to some extent victim of the abstract character of the notion of freedom. In a regime like the Nazi regime, people are certainly not free, but not having freedom doesn't mean not having power.

Cahiers: Historical discourse has the most impact in the film and television arena, with television being entirely controlled by power. This implies a political responsibility. It seems to us that people are becoming more and more aware of this. Over the last few years there has been more and more talk about history, politics, and struggle.

Foucault: There's a very interesting battle for and around history taking place at present. The intention is to encode and to suppress what I have termed "popular memory" and also to impose and propose to people a framework for interpreting the present. Popular struggles, right up until 1968, were part of folklore. For some people they weren't even part of their immediate reality. Since 1968, all popular struggles, whether they have taken place in South America or in Africa, have found a resonance and a sympathetic response. So we can no longer keep up this separation, this kind of geographical "quarantine." In our system popular struggles have become not just a news item but something that might be possible. So once again, they have to be kept at a distance. How? Not by providing a direct interpretation, which would mean that all sorts of denials would need to be made, but by offering a historical interpretation of past popular struggles in our country in order to show that they didn't in fact exist. Before 1968, it was: "It won't happen because it only happens somewhere else"; now it's: "It won't happen, because it never happened! And even when you look at something like the Resistance, which so many have dreamt about, look closely—nothing. It's empty, it rings hollow!" It's another way of saying: "Don't worry about Chile, it's the same thing there: the Chilean peasants couldn't care less. In France too: what can a few malcontents do? It doesn't affect the general population."

Cahiers: What's important for us, when we react to all this and against it, is not just being content to reestablish the truth, to say about the maquis, for example: "No, I was there, it wasn't like that!" We think that if you're going to carry on any effective ideological struggle on the kind of terrain that these films occupy, you need a framework of reference—a positive frame of reference—that is broader and vaster. For instance, for many people, this consists in reclaiming "the history of France." It's from this perspective that we read *I, Pierre Rivière*[7] with a great deal of interest, because we realized that, ultimately and paradoxically, it was useful for us in providing an account of *Lacombe, Lucien*, and that the comparison was not unproductive. For example, there is a significant difference in that Pierre Rivière is a man who writes, who executes a murder, and who has a quite extraordinary memory. Malle, on the other hand, treats his hero as a half-wit, as someone who goes through everything—history, war, collaboration—without gaining anything from his experience. This is where the theme of memory, of popular memory, can help make a division between someone like Pierre Rivière and the character created by Malle and Modiano.[8] Rivière speaks, even if he has no voice and is compelled to kill in order to qualify for the right to speak. And Lucien Lacombe, by not making anything of what happens to him, proves precisely that there's nothing that's worth remembering. It's a pity that you haven't seen *The Night of San Juan*.[9] This is a Bolivian film that was made explicitly as evidence in a case. The film, which has been circulating around the globe (with the exception of Bolivia, because of the regime), is played by the very people who were involved in the real drama that it re-creates (a miners' strike and its bloody repression). They themselves take charge of their own representation, so that no one can forget.

It's interesting to see that, at the base level, every film functions as a potential archive and that you can take up this idea in the context of struggle and move to a more advanced stage, to the point where people can organize their own film as evidence. This can be conceptualized in two radically different ways: first, film puts power center stage, representing the victims of power. The victims are the exploited classes who, without the assistance of a film production and distribution network and with very few technical resources, take charge of their own representation and make their case for history. This is similar to the way in which Pierre Rivière made his own case, that is, he began to write, knowing that sooner or later he was going to appear in court and that everyone needed to understand what he had to say.

What is important in *The Night of San Juan* is that the impetus effectively came from the people. The director became aware of this impetus after conducting an inquiry. It was the people who experienced the event who wanted it committed to memory.

Foucault: The people established their own internal archives.

Cahiers: The difference between *Pierre Rivière* and *Lacombe, Lucien* is that Pierre Rivière did everything he could to ensure that his story would be discussed after his death. Whereas, in Lacombe's case, even if he had been a real person or someone who might have existed, he's only the object of somebody else's discourse, for ends that are not his own.

There are two things at work in film at present, and historical documents have an important role. They play a very important role in *Ein Leben Lang* (1940),[10] for example. Or again, in the films of Marcel Ophüls or Harris and Sedouy,[11] it's moving to see the reality of Duclos in action in 1936 and in 1939.[12] On the other hand, there are fictional characters who very effectively condense social relationships and relationships to history at a given moment in history. This is why *Lacombe, Lucien* works so well. Lacombe is a Frenchman during the Occupation, a guy with a concrete relationship to Nazism, to the countryside, and to local authorities, and so on. We shouldn't ignore this way of personifying history, of enacting it through a character or a set of characters who embody a privileged relationship to power at a given time.

There are plenty of unknown figures in the history of the workers' movement. There are many heroes in the history of the working class who have been completely forgotten. And I think that there's a real issue here. Marxism doesn't need to keep making films on Lenin; there have been enough.

Foucault: What you say is important. Ignorance of history is a characteristic of many Marxists today. All these people who spend their time talking about the ignorance of history are only capable of producing commentary on texts: What did Marx say? Did Marx really say this? But what is Marxism, except another way of analyzing history itself? In my opinion, the left in France has no real understanding of history. It used to have. In the nineteenth century, you might say that Michelet represented the left for a while. There was Jaurès too, then a kind of tradition of left-wing Social Democrat historians developed after that (Mathiez, etc.). This has now been reduced to a trickle. It could have been a great movement that included writers and filmmakers. There is still Aragon and *Les Cloches de Bâle*,[13] which is a great historical novel. But this is a relatively small thing compared to what it could have been in a society where, after all, intellectuals can be described as being pretty much impregnated with Marxism.

Cahiers: Film offers something new in this regard: history captured "live." What relation do people in America have to history, watching the Vietnam War on television every night over dinner?

Foucault: As soon as you start seeing images of war every night, war becomes totally bearable. That is, perfectly boring; you really want to watch something else. But the instant it becomes boring, it becomes tolerable. You don't even watch. So how do we make sure that these filmed events are kept active as an important historical moment?

Cahiers: Have you seen René Allio's 1972 film, *The French Calvinists*?

Foucault: Yes, I really liked it. Historically, it's faultless. It's well-made, it's intelligent, and it clarifies a lot of things.

Cahiers: I think we need to go in this direction when we're making films. To go back to the films we were talking about at the beginning, we need to raise the problem of the far left's confusion in relation to certain aspects, particularly the sexual aspects of *Lacombe, Lucien* or *The Night Porter*. How might this confusion benefit the right?

Foucault: I'm in rather a quandary with respect to what you describe as the far left. I'm not at all sure that it still exists. There are an enormous number of things the far left has done since 1968 that need to be taken stock of, both negatively and positively. It's true that the far left has been the means of dissemination of a whole range of important ideas in relation to sexuality, women, homosexuality, psychiatry, housing, and medicine. It has also been the means of disseminating modes of action that are of continuing importance. The far left has been important both in terms of forms of action as well as in terms of issues. But there is also a negative balance in terms of certain Stalinist, terrorist, and organizational practices. There has also been a misunderstanding of the widespread and profound processes that led to the thirteen million votes for Mitterrand. These have always been overlooked on the pretext that it was about the politics of politicians or about party politics. Numerous aspects have been overlooked; notably, that the desire to defeat the right has been a very important political factor for the masses for a number of months, even years. The far left was not aware of this desire because of a false definition of the masses and a false apprehension of what the desire to win was all about. It preferred not to take the risk of winning at all, citing the risk of a hijacked victory. Defeat, at least, can't be exploited. Personally, I'm not so sure.

4

MARGUERITE DURAS

Memory Without Remembering

ichel Foucault: The idea of discussing Marguerite Duras has been worrying me somewhat since this morning. Reading her work and seeing her films always leaves me with a very strong impression. Marguerite Duras's work remains very intensely present for me, no matter how long it is since I've read it, but then suddenly, as soon as I start talking about her work, I have the impression that it's all slipping away from me. It's like a kind of naked force that you slide up against, which your hands can't get a grip around. It's the presence of this force, this smooth and mobile force, this presence that is fleeting at the same time, that prevents me from speaking, and which is probably what I find attractive about it.

Hélène Cixous: I had the same kind of feeling just before. I picked up all of Marguerite Duras's texts, which I have read several times before, thinking, naively, that I knew them well. But we can't really know Marguerite Duras, we can't pin her down. I say to myself, I know and I've read, but then I realize that I haven't "retained" anything. That's perhaps what it is: there is a Duras effect, and this Duras effect means that something very powerful passes through you. This is what her text is meant to do perhaps: it flows away and can't be retained, like her characters who always drift away from themselves. So what

I "retain" is this impression. This has been instructive. She has taught me something about a certain outpouring that almost goes beyond the text, even if this is an effect of writing.

I've wondered about the mystery of what it is in her texts that hooks you in. There are points in her texts that, for me in any case, are related to and linked to *seduction*: it hooks you in very strongly, it takes hold of you, it gains the upper hand. For example, one image from one of her books has really stuck with me: it's the image of the plunging neckline of a woman's blouse in *Moderato cantabile*.[1] I projected a breast from which rose a flower—but I don't know if that's what you actually saw. My whole attention fixated on that; you reach into the woman, and you are held within her, by this flower and by this breast. And I thought, ultimately, the whole book has been written as if it was leading up to this image that really takes hold of you. So the book's space, which at the same time is desert, sand, beach, and disintegrated life, leads us to something very small, which at the same time is tremendously valorized: it is something that is transmitted like lightning through the body and the flesh. That's what Marguerite Duras has invented; it's what I would call the art of poverty. Wealth and monuments are all abandoned little by little as we gradually advance through her work. I think she's aware of this: she strips more and more away, she adds less and less in the way of settings, furnishings, and objects, and then it becomes so impoverished that at the end something is left that remains, records, and collects and gathers together everything that doesn't want to die. It's as if all our desires are reinvested in something tiny that becomes as big as love. I won't say the universe, but love. And this love is this nothing, which is everything. Don't you think that's how it works?

Foucault: Yes. I think you're absolutely right. And your analysis is really wonderful. We can see rather well what has underpinned a work like this from Blanchot—who is very important for her I think—through to Beckett. It's this art of poverty, or what might be called memory without remembering. In Blanchot, as in Duras, this discourse exists entirely within the dimension of memory, of a memory that has been completely cleansed of all remembering, which is nothing more than a kind of fog, perpetually referring to memory, a memory of memory, with each memory erasing all remembering, and so on indefinitely.

So how can work like this abruptly appear in film, producing a cinematic output, which is, I think, just as important as the literary work? And then how does it arrive with images and characters at this art of poverty, at this memory without remembering, at this kind of outside that ultimately only crystallizes in a gesture or in a gaze?

Cixous: I think that her other strength is her relationship to the gaze. This is what first struck me in my reading. I didn't find Marguerite Duras particularly easy to read to begin with. I read her with resistance as I didn't like the position she put me in. I was resolved not to occupy, without some displeasure, the position she uses to attract and "put" people in. I had to overcome that. I think it's her relationship to the gaze. You said memory without remembering. That's it. The work that she does is a work of loss, as if the loss never comes to an end: it's very paradoxical. It's as if the loss never goes far enough; you always have more to lose. Her work always goes in that direction.

Yes, her memory without remembering is as if the memory wasn't able to appear, as if the past was so past that, in order to remember, you had to go back to the past. *Be* past. The past doesn't come back. This is something monstrous; it's impossible to conceptualize and yet that's what it is, I think. And how does this emerge in the image? It produces a vision of extreme intensity, because it's a vision that can't come back to look again. It's a vision that can't hold on to anything. You have all these people who are being "watched"; that too was one of the things that bothered me, before I managed to accept what Duras was asking for: that is, the most extreme passivity. One character after another comes forward with a gaze that bears down on the other, a demand that asks for nothing. She has some really lovely phrases, which are always passive phrases: someone is being watched. "She" is being watched, but she doesn't know that she's being watched. On the one hand, a gaze bears down on a subject who doesn't respond, a subject who is so bereft of images that he or she has nothing with which to reflect a gaze. On the other hand, the person who's doing the looking is someone who is also so impoverished and so cut off that they would want to be able to grasp what it is to look, they want to capture it. It's always the same, this sand that drifts.

Foucault: Would you say it drifts in the same way in the films as it does in the books? In the books, there's a perpetual nullification as soon as anything like a presence begins to take shape. Presence hides behind its own actions, its own view on things, and it dissolves. Nothing remains except a kind of fragment that refers to another fragment, and the slightest appeal to any memory is annulled. In the films, on the other hand, it seems to me that it's a matter of sudden emergences. Emergences without presence, but you see the emergence of a gesture, the emergence of an eye: a character who comes out of the fog. I'm thinking of Francis Bacon. It seems to me that her films are loosely related to Bacon just as her novels are to Blanchot: on the one hand, nullification; on the other, emergences.

Cixous: The two go together. I've only seen two of her films. I've seen *Détruire dit-elle* (1969) and *India Song* (1975), which are both very different.

Foucault: Tell me about *India Song*. I haven't seen it.

Cixous: I loved this film and yet I feel that it escaped me. What's left of *India Song* for me? *India Song* is a film that has a quite unique dimension, even for Marguerite Duras, because it's a film where you find an absolutely intense enjoyment [*jouissance*]. Marguerite Duras has succeeded in pulling off something fabulous: she has shown on screen what I consider to be the most profound fantasy of every human being. She set herself the task of seeing what she has always been looking at without being able to pin it down. There's one thing that we haven't talked about, and that is very important to me: everything that Marguerite Duras writes about, all that precise stripping away and loss, is also fantastically erotic. This is because Marguerite Duras is someone who is absolutely in thrall. I can't help but say that it's "her" because she's the driving force behind it. Being in thrall goes hand in hand with poverty. She's in thrall as if she has been caught by something or someone, a someone or something that is absolutely mysterious and means that the rest of the world turns to dust. There's nothing else left.

It could be a religious fascination, and there is indeed a religious dimension to her work, except that what fascinates her is discovered little by little. Indeed, I think that she herself is in the process of discovering it or allowing it to be discovered. It's a mixture of eroticism that involves women's flesh and then death. It runs the gamut of that overwhelming and beautiful something that is indefinable in women. And it all merges together. Then it's lost again. It's as if death has swallowed life and beauty with the terrible tenderness of love. It's as if death *loved* life.

It's as if she saw how we give ourselves in *India Song*, it's as if she finally saw "it," that thing that has always fascinated her. And it's a very dark sort of sun. At the center, there's the unforgettable woman, who attracts all desires in every book. From text to text, everything rushes into this chasm. It's a female body that doesn't know itself but knows something obscurely, knows darkness, knows death. She's there, she's embodied, and once again there is this inverted sun, since all the rays—male rays—come to be pulled into the chasm toward which she radiates. Obviously, the films shift the impact of the books, as there are faces in the films. You can't help but see them, whereas in the books, they are always shown as not visible or as already dispersed.

Foucault: Yes, that's it. The visibility in the films is still not a presence. I don't know if Lonsdale acts in this film. I imagine he does, because he is such a good actor for Marguerite Duras. There is in him a kind of fog-like thickness. We don't know what his form is. We don't know what his face is like. Does Lonsdale have a nose, does Lonsdale have a chin? Does he have a smile? I really don't know. He is thick and solid like a formless fog, and out of this fog come rumblings from who knows where, rumblings that are his voice, or again his gestures, which are not attached to anything, which come through the screen toward you. A kind of third dimension, where only the third dimension is left without the other two to support it, so that it's always in front of you, it's always between the screen and you, it's never either on or in the screen. That's what Lonsdale is. It seems to me that Lonsdale is absolutely one with Duras's text, or rather with this mixture of text/image.

Cixous: He is indeed the text itself (in) person. He is uncertainty in person, or at least the uncertain in person. But uncertainty is already too strong a word. And, indeed, he's there. He is wonderful as someone lost, as he *is* lost.

Foucault: He is cotton and lead at the same time.

Cixous: And he has this voice. He is gifted with a voice. This is very important; it's as if there's been a shift in emphasis. What in the book is in the gaze, a gaze that is always cut short, a gaze that doesn't reach its target, in the film becomes a voice, because after all *India Song* is *song*, it's singing.

When you see *India Song*, you get the impression that the visual is completely interwoven into a tapestry of continuous voice: this visual, which is at once very beautiful and very erotic, but also very vague, makes it completely seductive, because it is there without being there.

Her work with the voices is marvelous, producing these wonderful wandering and disembodied voices. There are bodies without voice and voices without bodies. The voices are like birds constantly around us, very beautiful and very refined. They are very gentle voices, like the voices of women in a choir, or rather an antichoir; they are fluttering voices that come from somewhere else, and that somewhere else is obviously time. But this time is a time that cannot be recovered, and if you are not very careful, this voice leads to confusion, because it is reverberating now: it appears to be present, but, in reality, it's a voice from the past, telling a story that takes you back. The voices take what you see and send it back into a past that remains indeterminate.

Foucault: It's here that we come across something that's very powerful in Duras's novels, namely, what is traditionally called dialogue. Dialogues don't occupy the same position, the same status, and are not integrated in the same way in Marguerite Duras's novels as they are in traditional novels. The dialogue is not included in the plot, it doesn't come to break up the story; it's always in a very uncertain position, running through it, contradicting it, arriving from below or above. It's absolutely not at the same level as the text, and it produces a misty and floating effect around the parts that are not dialogue and what looks like it's being spoken by the author.

Cixous: That's quite true. This originates from the issues or affects in her texts, because, ultimately, what is pursued and yearned for through all these texts is the possibility of speaking *from somewhere.* It's this problem of time, memory, history, the past, and so on. It starts *from an absolutely infinite and terrible despair*, which at the same time is a despair that has been cut short, a despair that cannot even be called despair, because it would then already be under control, and mourning would already be in progress. There's not even the possibility, or the will, to mourn. So instead of the dialogues that you would find in any other novel, there are exchanges. In spite of everything, they do manage to make an exchange somewhere, besides, that's what love is. And these exchanges are based on a mutual foundation of unhappiness and on their relationship to death, which one might say calls to them. This is the case in almost all her texts, but there is one exception. I advance this somewhat boldly, but it seems to me that there's one text that doesn't lead to the vast infinity into which everybody plummets, and that is *Destroy, She Said.*[2] Here, there is a kind of gaiety that emanates—a gaiety that emerges against a background of violence, of course— from those three strange beings, the trinity represented by Stein, Thor, and Alissa, who keep themselves apart from the others. They remain active while the others are passive or overwhelmed. There's something that constantly communicates and circulates, and which triumphs. There's laughter ending with the phrase "she said." It all ends with laughter and music.

Foucault: One has the impression that this is something unique in Marguerite Duras's work.

How does one describe this kind of exultation, this kind of laughter that goes around, something that can't exactly be described as gaiety? When you were talking about exchange earlier, I winced a little at the word "exchange" because there is no reciprocity; everything just circulates. It is rather like a game of pass the slipper, but a game where the slipper also possesses its own autonomy. Someone passes it on and the next person takes it, indeed they are obliged to take it, but what also happens in Marguerite Duras's game is that the slipper spontaneously leaps from hand to hand without either being responsible. In any case, it circulates. The slipper has its ruses, and these are the same ruses as those holding the slipper. There's a perpetual irony, something amusing that, against this background of what I think you are right to call despair, still makes the texts, the smiles, and actions sparkle, all shimmering a bit like the sea.

Cixous: You could say that about *Destroy, She Said*, where there's a terrible irony. I don't read the others as being amusing, but still, it might be me who's missing something. I read them as a kind of melancholy song, a song of death. If there's something amusing there, it is *episodic* and incidental. All those extraordinary social and sociocultural scenes, those embassy and cocktail scenes, which Duras really sinks her teeth into, are fake signifiers. But I don't see anything amusing in what happens between these people, between what remains of these people. I see something that isn't closed; I see a kind of infinite generosity. Infinite, because everybody is welcomed in poverty, all those who have lost everything are welcomed. It isn't closed off, it opens on to the infinite, but to an infinity of pain.

Foucault: "Amusing." You know, I hesitated over this word. I don't want to defend it. For me, it's not inconsistent with either "pain" or, indeed, history, and, well, certainly not with "suffering." There's something amusing in pain, something amusing in suffering and in death. Amusing, you know, in the sense of something strange, sharp, and elusive. "It's amusing," disturbing.

Cixous: It's your sensibility that perceives that. I see it as horror. That may be because I feel deeply threatened by Marguerite Duras's texts. I think, "I don't want anything to do with this." I don't want there to be people like that. For me, what is emphasized is impotence: an impotence that can only be redeemed—although it's not a matter of redemption. It's only tolerable to me personally because it's humble, because it deploys an extraordinary amount of love at the same time. This is what's wonderful.

You said before that the word "exchange" was not a good one; that's true. But they also touch each other through the poverty of language. Who? They? These human beings, these wanderers who reach out to each other across a vast land. They caress and gently brush against each other. This is deeply moving. What I like in her work is that this relation of touch exists all the time.

This is what I saw in *India Song*. I think I recall that Anne-Marie Stretter played the piano when she was young; in any case, she played music. And then she stops playing, and at the same time, she is surrounded by all these men, I don't know how many. Anyway, there are several. And they are all engulfed in her, but she isn't a fatal abyss because she doesn't mean any harm, and she doesn't take anything. But at the same time, without calling, she calls, because she has renounced everything, whereas they haven't as yet renounced everything as they still want *her*, they hold on to her and she holds on to nothing. And through her, they touch the void. What I mean, what remains open, what happens, and what this means is that she is *someone who no longer plays music*, she no longer allows herself what music gives you. She no longer allows herself the pleasure of music, no longer allows herself a voice. *She has become silence*, and because she has created silence, she is someone who is able to listen to others. Within her is the space, the opening that means that she can hear others fall silent, or scream like the vice-consul. There are those who scream and those who say nothing. She hears words, she hears the desire of others, she hears the unhappiness of others. And that, ultimately, is the power of her love.

She has a capacity for listening (obviously not psychoanalytic listening, which erects a wall that echoes back what you say. You aren't listened to, you listen to yourself. Maybe I'm wrong about this.).

She is like the sea into which she eventually vanishes, the infinite. You throw something. She catches it. Her body is like the threshold of infinity; you feel that this something is caught because it has gone through a flesh that can be touched, and then it travels on to infinity. That's what despair is: you go through love and then you fall into death. Marguerite Duras is someone who has an extremely powerful unconscious. She is a "blind" woman. This has always fascinated me; I believe who I see. I believe Marguerite Duras as she presents herself to me. She "sees" nothing, and besides, when she doesn't see faces, I think that it really is because she doesn't see, but at the same time, there is someone in her who does see. We need to see how she sees. I'm not able to see where the division between the conscious and the unconscious is in Duras. I don't know where the boundary is. I admire in her precisely the fact that in the end she is so blind that everything is always abruptly discovered. Suddenly, she *sees*, something that has always been there. And it this "suddenly" that allows her to write.

Foucault: Something appears in her books: is it because she has seen it, or is it because she has touched it? I think this is undecidable. She has managed to define a kind of intersecting plane between the visible and the tactile, which is pretty extraordinary.

Cixous: I think this happens precisely at the point where it is cut short. Because it's always cut short. The gaze is cut short, if you like, at that point on the plane where the gaze is, indeed, broken off by touch.

Foucault: Earlier you said that basically she's blind. I think this is profoundly true. She's blind, almost in the technical sense of the term, that is, touch is indeed framed by a kind of possible visibility, or again her ways of seeing are through touch. And I don't mean that a blind person substitutes touch for vision; she sees with her touch, and what she touches produces the visible. And I wonder if it's not this profound blindness that is at work in what she does.

Cixous: And which is really what is incalculable about her.

Foucault: Perhaps this also corresponds with what we can say about the exterior. On the one hand, it's true that you can never get inside either the characters or even what happens between them, and yet there is always another exterior in relation to them. The beggar woman, for example. What are those cries, what are those things happening that are strongly signaled as being exterior and as such have a particular effect on the characters? This is also what takes place between them. So there are three exteriors: the one we inhabit, the one that is defined as the one the characters inhabit, and then this third exterior where they intersect. The blind person is always exterior to everything. Her eyes aren't closed; on the contrary, she's the one who has no interior.

Cixous: And this is where it all comes back to, or anyway, where it begins—because, in a certain way, she controls things in an astounding way, in a way that we just don't know the origins of. Where does this control come from? It comes through the voice. It's there where you can hear, and she has a good ear even if her gaze is cut short; she has a good ear, and that's what makes up for it, that's where the outside comes back in, the voice is what breaks through.

5

PAUL'S STORY

The Story of Jonah

I saw *The Story of Paul* (1975) and rubbed my eyes. I recognized the faces of professional actors. And yet the film I saw was not *like* the asylum, it *was* the asylum. I wondered whether the actors had perhaps spent several weeks or months in a psychiatric hospital, mixing with those who were ill, studying what happened, observing movements, eavesdropping, noting all those dialogues without an echo. René Féret did the opposite. He put professional actors into the empty shell of an asylum, dividing them up between its walls, doors, iron bedsteads, wards, and Ping-Pong tables. He made them take on the age-old movements of the hospital and reconstructed the old hierarchies, both visible and secret, of the madhouse. In short, he launched the machinery of the asylum, then asked his actors to just follow their own inclinations and their own angles. It's an amazing experiment with the strength and the molding effects of the asylum. The actors spontaneously became asylum flora and fauna in the hothouse in which they were placed, without any rule other than the form of psychiatric power. Both strange and familiar flora: the man in fits of laughter, the anxious questioner, the man murmuring his prayers, the man who is cured every month and who comes back every month. Everyone on his path, they constantly pass each other, but, like the lanes of the motorways that form flowers at city entrances, they never meet. These are the grand rituals of the asylum that Féret and his actors managed to reactivate—meals, card games, Ping-Pong—where the lines, movements, food, dishes, balls, dice, questions, complaints, and grimaces intersect with the speed and accuracy of lightning, and where, in spite of all this, "it just doesn't work." Antitheater, in short. These men needed all their talents (all, or almost all, with a background in theater), and the inevitable force of the asylum, to actually and voluntarily "act crazy" far from the stage.

Paul is admitted to the asylum. Neither sane nor insane, neither sick nor in good health, neither constrained nor a voluntary admission, neither anxious nor aggressive. Blank, empty, "apathetic," indifferent, and infinitely attentive, as if on the threshold of an initiation: soon to be inducted into the grand order of unreason. The long shot of his initial undressing is almost unbearable in its indiscretion. The madman of the Middle Ages was recognized by his bells and rags; that of the nineteenth century by his delirium and cries. Entry into madness today is through a silent, submissive, and exhaustive session of being stripped naked. Paul (played by Paul Allio) marks the point where all stupors intersect: his own stupor in the face of those frozen masks of madness that revolve around him, which signal to him, and one of which—which one? choice, chance, fate?—will one day become his. There is the stupor of the madmen who are watching him: a body without a species, patient without a category, companion without a name, without a diagnosis, with no role, no job, which the madmen will capture in the net of their own madness and offer to the doctors when he is finally worthy of a pathological baptism. There's a stupor that is also injected into his veins by the watchful gaze of the attendants, the words

of the doctors who talk about him, above him, without addressing him, and by the medications that he is forced to take. Our
own stupor at seeing madness welling up in the solidity of a
body that doesn't move, through the features of a face that systematically remains "expressionless." Paul Allio's performance
is remarkable. He eventually seems to dissolve and take control
of the water that haunts his dreams, water that he may once
have wanted to drown himself in and that now tranquilly fills
the grand psychiatric aquarium.

There is a mildness to the asylum (at least since the neurolep-
tics), although it is still furrowed by violence, occasionally swept
away by whirlwinds and shot through with lightning. The pinnacle of this gentleness and its symbol is food. The asylum
is still about confinement and exclusion perhaps, but now
added to this is ingestion. As if to the old traditional hospital
laws: "You will not move, you will not cry out," was added
this one: "You will swallow." You will swallow your medications,
you will swallow your meals, you will swallow our care, our
promises and threats, you will swallow your relatives' visits. You
will swallow the provisions that your mother smuggles in every
week in her bag, provisions that she insists on bringing you as a
ritual offering to "her" patient and which you must eat in front
of her for her delight, in communion with this illness that
belongs to both of you, an illness that marks the most intense
point of your relationship and in which she has invested, poor
thing, all her love for you. Today, asylum inmates are no longer
starving behind bars: they are doomed to ingestion. Paul's story
is a story of absorption, an open and closed mouth, meals taken
and rejected, the sound of plates and glasses. As René Féret has
clearly seen, the function of food in hospital today is not to pro-
mote recovery. Between an unwanted madness and an unhoped
for cure, the docile swallowing of food reveals the prized figure

of the "good patient." In the asylum, the patient who eats well is the long-term inmate who satisfies everyone. The essential part of the introduction to hospital is the food test. The film culminates in an extraordinary feat of "crêpe swallowing," marking a digestive prowess and final ritual through which Paul becomes the "number one" of the mentally ill to the satisfaction of all—relatives, attendants, and especially other patients. The swallower is swallowed; the story of Paul, the story of Jonah.

We had *Family Life* (1971);[1] now we have *Hospital Life*. But René Féret's film, in its great beauty and rigor, makes me think above all of those festivals of fools, such as they still existed just a few years ago in some hospitals in Germany and Switzerland. On carnival day, the mad dressed up and went on a masked parade in the streets: to the embarrassed, somewhat frightened curiosity of spectators. The only day mad people were allowed to go out was for a laugh, to go crazy. In this film-experiment, René Féret has turned this festival upside down: he put the not mad in the madhouse and told them: let yourselves go, go crazy as far as circumstances and the logic of internment allow. And from this has emerged, in its true reality, the unyielding, repetitive, and ritual form of madness: madness, the most strictly regulated thing in the world.

6

THE NONDISCIPLINARY CAMERA
VERSUS SADE

érard Dupont: When you go to the movies, are you struck by the sadism of some recent films, films that are set in hospitals or in a fake prison, as in Pasolini's most recent film?[1]

Michel Foucault: Actually, I have been struck—at least until recently—by the absence of sadism and by the absence of Sade. Besides, these two things are not equivalent. You can have Sade without sadism and sadism without Sade. But let's leave aside the problem of sadism, which is trickier, and focus on Sade. I believe that there's nothing more allergic to film than the work of Sade. Among the many reasons for this, there is this one to begin with: the meticulousness, the ritual, the rigorous forms of ceremony that you find in all of Sade's work excludes anything that the supplementary play of the camera might contribute. The slightest addition, the slightest suppression, the tiniest ornament are intolerable. Rather than free-flowing fantasy you have carefully planned regimentation. The moment anything goes missing or is superimposed, all is lost. There's no place for images. The blank spaces must only be filled by desires and bodies.

Dupont: In the first part of Jodorowsky's *El Topo* (1970), there's a bloody orgy with a fairly significant quota of body dismemberment. Isn't sadism in film primarily a way of treating actors and their bodies? And aren't women in particular (mis) treated as appendages of the male body in film?

Foucault: The way we treat the body in contemporary cinema is something very new. Look at the kisses, the faces, the lips, the cheeks, the eyelids, the teeth in a film like Werner Schroeter's *The Death of Maria Malibran* (1972). Calling that sadism seems to me quite wrong, unless you invoke a vague kind of psychoanalysis involving the partial object, the fragmented body, or the vagina dentata. You have to resort to a fairly vulgar Freudianism to fall back on sadism as a way of describing this way of celebrating bodies and their wonders. What Schroeter does with a face, a cheekbone, lips, and an expression in the eyes has nothing to do with sadism. It is more a reduction, a granulation of the body, a kind of autonomous exaltation of its smallest parts, of the minutest potentials of a fragment of the body. The body becomes anarchic, and hierarchies, localizations, and designations, organicity, if you like, all come undone. In sadism, however, it is the organ as such that is the object of obsession. You have an eye that sees; I'll tear it out. You have a tongue that I have taken between my lips and bitten; I am cutting it out. With those eyes, you can no longer see, with that tongue, you can no longer eat or speak. The body for Sade is still strongly organic and anchored in that hierarchy, the difference being, of course, that the hierarchy is not organized, as in the old fable, from the head down but begins with the genitals.

In a number of contemporary films, however, the way of liberating the body from itself is quite different. The aim is precisely to dismantle this organicity: this is no longer a tongue, this is completely different from a tongue coming out of a mouth, this is not the organ of a mouth that has been desecrated and intended for somebody else's pleasure. It is an "unnameable" and "unusable" thing, existing beyond all programs of desire; it is a body rendered entirely plastic by pleasure: something that opens, stretches, throbs, beats, and gapes. When we see two women embrace in *The Death of Maria Malibran*, we see dunes, a desert caravan, a voracious advancing flower, insect mandibles, a grassy crevice. All of that is antisadism. The cruel science of desire has nothing to do with these shapeless pseudopods, which are the slow movements of pleasure-pain.

Dupont: Have you seen those films called Snuff movies in New York (in American slang, to snuff: to kill) where a woman is cut into pieces?

Foucault: No, apparently, I believe, the woman really is dismembered alive.

Dupont: It's purely visual, without words. A cold medium, compared with film, which is a hot medium. No literary reflection on the body: it is just a body dying.

Foucault: This is no longer cinema. It's something that takes place in private erotic circuits with the sole function of igniting desire. It's simply a matter, as Americans say, of being *turned on* by that kind of capacity for stimulation that can only come from images, something that is no less powerful than real life stimulation—only different.

Dupont: Perhaps we could see the camera as the dominatrix who victimizes the actor's body? I am thinking of Marilyn Monroe constantly falling at Tony Curtis's feet in *Some Like It Hot* (1959). Surely the actress must have experienced these sequences as sadistic.

Foucault: The relationship between the actor and the camera you are talking about in this film still appears very traditional to me. You can see it in theater, with the actors taking the sacrifice of the hero on themselves and realizing it within their own bodies. What I think is new in the kind of films I mentioned earlier is the discovery and exploration of the body using the camera. I imagine that shooting these films must be really intense. There is both a calculated and an unpredictable encounter between the body and the camera, revealing something, making an angle appear, a volume, a curve following a track, a line, perhaps a wrinkle. And then, suddenly, the body is reconfigured, becomes a landscape, a caravan, a storm, a mountain of sand, and so on. This is the opposite of sadism, which dismembers the whole. Schroeter's camera doesn't break down the body to meet the ends of desire but kneads the body like dough and makes images emerge from it that are images of pleasure and for pleasure. The constantly unpredictable encounter between the camera (and its pleasure) and the body (and its own pulsations of pleasure) gives rise to these images, pleasures with multiple entry points.

Sadism was anatomically obedient, and if it went on the rampage, it was within the confines of a very rational manual of anatomy. There is no organic madness in Sade. Trying to adapt Sade, this meticulous anatomist, into precise images doesn't work. Either Sade disappears or you make the *cinéma de papa*.

Dupont: It's a *cinéma de papa* quite literally in view of a recent association, in terms of a retro revival, between fascism and sadism, for instance, Liliana Cavani's *The Night Porter* (1974) and Pasolini's *Salò* (1975). But this representation is not actually historical. Bodies are decked out in old period costumes. They try to convince us that Himmler's henchmen correspond to the Duke, the Bishop, and His Excellency in Sade's texts.

Foucault: This is a total historical error. Nazism was not invented by grand twentieth-century erotic madmen but by the most sinister, boring, and disgusting petty-bourgeois imaginable.

Himmler was some kind of agriculturalist who married a nurse. We need to understand that concentration camps were the product of the joint imagination of a hospital nurse and a chicken farmer. A hospital combined with a barnyard: that's the fantasy that was behind the concentration camps. Millions of people were killed there, so I'm not saying this to minimize the blame in relation to this enterprise, but precisely to remove the glamour of all the erotic values that some have sought to superimpose on it. The Nazis were cleaning ladies in the bad sense of the term. They worked with dusters and brooms, trying to purge society of everything they defined as pus, dirt, and garbage: syphilitics, homosexuals, Jews, those of impure blood, blacks, the mad. This was the disgusting petty-bourgeois dream of racial cleanliness that underlay the Nazi dream: a total absence of eros.

That said, it's quite possible that erotic relations were produced locally within this structure by the physical confrontation between the torturer and the victim. But this was accidental.

The problem is trying to understand why we imagine today that we access certain erotic fantasies via Nazism. Why are these boots, these caps, these eagles the subject of such frequent infatuation, particularly in the United States? Is it something to do with our current incapacity to truly live out this great wonder of the fragmented body, which makes us fall back on a meticulous, disciplinary, anatomical sadism? Is this sad fable of a recent political apocalypse the only language we have to transcribe this great pleasure of the body in explosion? Are we unable to interpret the intensity of the present except as the end of the world in a concentration camp? How impoverished our bank of images must be! And how urgent it is to build a new one instead of moaning about "alienation" and reviling the "spectacle."

Dupont: Sade is seen by some directors rather like the maid, the night porter, the window cleaner. At the end of Pasolini's film we see torture through a window. The window cleaner sees what is happening in a distant medieval courtyard through the window.

Foucault: You know, I'm not in favor of Sade's total consecration. At the end of the day, I would be quite happy to acknowledge that Sade formulated an eroticism that was a perfect fit for a disciplinary society: a regulated, anatomical, hierarchical society, with its carefully distributed time, its partitioned spaces, its obediences, and its surveillances. We need to leave this behind and Sade's eroticism with it. We need to accept the body, with its elements, surfaces, volumes, and mass and invent a nondisciplinary eroticism: an eroticism of the body in a volatile and diffuse state, with its chance encounters and uncalculated pleasures. What annoys me in recent films is that they use a certain number of elements that resurrect a disciplinary type of eroticism through the employment of Nazi themes. This is Sade's model perhaps. So much for Sade's literary canonization and so much for Sade; he's boring, he's a disciplinarian, a sex sergeant. He's an accountant who keeps a tally of sex and that's all.

7

THE ASYLUM AND THE CARNIVAL

ichel Foucault: When I saw your film, I rubbed my eyes. I rubbed my eyes, because I recognized the professional actors, yet what I saw in the film, I have to say, was not *like* the asylum, it *was* the asylum. I wondered whether your actors had perhaps spent several weeks or months in an asylum studying what happened, observing movements, listening to dialogues. You told me they'd done nothing of the sort, that in fact you had left your actors to follow a kind of path, thread, and the inclinations you had identified in them, and it was in working with them in this way that they were able to arrive at these characters who might typically belong to the asylum. Is this how it happened?

René Féret: We didn't need the actors to go on placements in psychiatric hospitals, but right from the film's conception, while writing the script for the film, before it was made, the team that was meeting was able to draw on the actual experiences of people who had been patients in asylums. Right from the outset, we wanted to construct a film from the point of view of a group of mad people. In studying these real experiences, we were able to reflect on the asylum, and the actors immediately became involved. I wrote for them based on the intimate knowledge I had of them. During the fortnight of rehearsals, they were placed in the settings, costumes, and accessories specific to an asylum, and using a video recorder, we were able to control, enrich, and develop the themes we had elaborated. The actors experienced the actual conditions of an asylum.

Foucault: You took the actors, put them into a space, into a system of coexistence, gave them asylum clothes, and let them follow their own inclination. If you took mentally ill people, dressed them, divided them up, and let them follow their own inclination in the way you have done, you'd end up with the same thing. The space of the asylum, its walls, its system of coexistence and hierarchy, produce a specific effect, and you can set these things in motion, you can make them appear in the same way in someone who is ill, in someone who is in a state of terrible anxiety, or in somebody who is just doing his job as an actor for a living. So this is an amazing experiment with the strength and plastic effects of the asylum's power. The way these characters behave, in such typical and stereotypical ways, is not, strictly speaking, indicative of symptoms or illness. They are the flora and fauna of asylums: the laughing man, with his sardonic laughter and his sometimes good-natured, sometimes anxious agitation, the anxious questioner, the man murmuring his prayers. All these people follow their own paths, which don't really intersect. It's a bit like those motorways, which look as though they intersect when you are viewing them from above, but which in fact pass above or below each other, in such a way that they never truly meet. Each occupies his or her own lane, crossing others but not meeting, but taken together in their pseudointersections these solitary lanes form "scenes" that are not really about communication but more about juxtaposition and solitude: Ping-Pong, card games, and meals. You are going to encounter some criticism in relation to the problem of the doctors, because they are caricatures. They are perhaps the only characters who are caricatures (the attendants aren't). The cavalcades through the wards, the cross-examinations that don't wait for responses are all grotesque. This doesn't match the reality of medical practice in asylums.

Féret: When we were preparing the film, we talked a lot about the role of the doctors, and it's true that some doctors who have seen the film are not entirely happy. The difference between the portrayal of the attendants and the doctors is to do with the fact that the attendants and the patients are two groups who flirt a little with each other, probably because they have more to do with each other and, in any case, in the film, they belong to the same social class. It's different when it comes to the doctors, especially as we have shown them from the patients' perspective. The film shows them as they appear to the patients with their power, their knowledge, and their intermittent visits. In the face of the objective reality of physicians' practice, we have developed a subjective perception from the patients' point of view.

Foucault: In short, what you wanted to show is that it's sufficient for medical power to be administered in a homeopathic dose. For the system to crystallize, it's enough for the doctor to drop in, ask a question, give an order. It's the tiny keystone that holds everything together. In a way, the doctors are seen from below, from the frog's perspective as Nietzsche would have it. The frog sees the world from the bottom up, so it's this personage who is present through all their effects in the asylum and yet always absent: a personage who is at once inaccessible, elusive, and enigmatic, with enormous feet and hands, a microscopic head, and a loudspeaker voice, a personage both all-powerful yet always ignored.

Féret: Some people have criticized me, saying that I was simply happy to describe or, in describing, I didn't seem to take a position, that I didn't show the causes or the solutions and only described the effects, that I didn't have a constructive attitude in dealing with this problem.

Foucault: You know, I think describing is already something important. And you've done more than that. Do you remember those experiments conducted in California where a number of students judged to be mentally sound were sent to a number of hospitals with false medical diagnoses? The idea was to see how long it would take for them to be recognized as healthy. They were immediately recognized as healthy by those who were ill, but it took medical staff several weeks. Personally, I believe that you've taken people who were sane, reconstructed the environment of the asylum around them, and then shown what happens. I would say this is a highly constructive experiment, because from here we can understand a whole series of mechanisms and effects that are specific to the institution of the asylum. An experiment like this with the actual effects of that fiction that is asylum has never been undertaken before.

Féret: I wanted to place Paul's subjective experience at the center of this "objective" experiment, allowing viewers to enter into the asylum themselves.

Foucault: The character is no more than a blank page. He has different circles that spin above his head. Immediately around him, around his bed, there's the circle of those who are ill, and standing a little above this is the circle of attendants, and then at the very top, sailing through the clouds, are the doctors. We know absolutely nothing about what actually brought him to the asylum, except for the recurring shots of water, which, I think, might refer to the suicide he attempted or wanted to commit. I think it might also point to the insular character of the asylum: water has been crossed and he is now in the middle of this water, and every time he leaves the asylum while sleeping and dreaming, he returns to this isolating water. This water is both a mark of his subjectivity and a reflection of the film's perspective.

Féret: The shots of water do indeed have the meanings you attribute to them. They also refer to Paul's problems, which will never be dealt with inside the asylum. They appear in moments of crisis, and the film ends with a long shot of water that says nothing more and can't say anything further in a place where Paul's problems can in no way be addressed, understood, or unraveled.

Foucault: The asylum itself takes on the nature of water: water that sends you to sleep and water that sleeps. Since the introduction of neuroleptic medication, there has been a gentleness about the asylum. I wouldn't say that violence no longer exists—indeed you have shown some of this violence. Every now and then in the midst of this cozy atmosphere, in the midst of this kind of spent storm, thunder, lightning, and brawls erupt. But there is a great gentleness about the asylum, and the pinnacle of this gentleness is food. In traditional mythology, the asylum was a place of violent repression at the same time as it was also a place of physical destitution, deficiency, penury, hunger, emaciation, and so on; starving people behind bars. Paul's mother comes with food, and indeed everybody arrives with shopping bags full of oranges, cakes, and chocolates, coming to feed the inmates, as if to compensate for confinement and its shortcomings. But this attempt from the outside to make up for the inside is redundant, because, as I think you have clearly demonstrated, everything in the asylum, when it comes down to it, revolves around absorption. Food and drugs must be absorbed; the good patient is the one who eats.

Féret: Paul's integration into the asylum can be read in terms of food from beginning to end. Paul begins by refusing all food; he is then punished and rejected by the patients themselves in the ward for "problem patients." In this ward, the other patients literally force Paul to swallow food. Paul, forced to fall in with this, returns to the first ward. He is finally accepted when he agrees to eat. He thus begins to be integrated into the institution.

Foucault: The wonderful scene with the crêpes seems to be the final turning point. It marks the moment when Paul accepts both the food his mother brings and the food provided by the hospital. He consequently comes to terms with the fact that he has been sent to the hospital by his family and also agrees to be a good patient at the hospital. The hospital works like a huge digestive apparatus, inside which people digest in their turn. It is a grand alimentary canal, Jonah's whale. The medication that has to be taken is both reward and guarantee, a mixture of pleasure and duty. Patients cluster around the table when the medications arrive. One patient even says: "What about me? Why do I only have one today, I had two yesterday, why do I only have one?"

The great beauty of your film, where each gesture is stripped down to its maximum intensity, is also underpinned by the terrible irony that everyone—patients and attendants—except perhaps the doctors—maintains with regard to this madness that provides them with employment.

Féret: There's no reason why humor shouldn't have a place in subject matter like this, and why not turn it into a show, since the actors' work is an essential element in all this? Sometimes people will laugh; they will also shudder I hope, and then they'll talk about it and think about it perhaps. The humor of the insane, the irony of the insane, do exist, and the actors approached all this with their own sense of humor and irony.

Foucault: You could argue that it's a little bit like the opposite of those festivals of fools that took place in certain psychiatric hospitals in Switzerland and I believe in some parts of Germany. On the day of the carnival, the mad dressed up and went into town, except those with serious conditions of course. They created a carnival, which the local population watched from a distance with fear. It was actually pretty awful that the only day they were allowed to go out en masse was the day they had to dress up and literally go crazy, just like those who are not mad go crazy. You've conducted the opposite experiment with the actors: "You're not mad, so go ahead and pretend to be mad and go crazy!"

Féret: "But be careful to go crazy according to the rules of the asylum in order to demonstrate its effects clearly."

Foucault: That's right, and "perform madness just as the rules say it should be performed and as you would perform it if you were inside an asylum." So this lends a funny side to it that in no way contradicts the reality of the asylum, and you can sense that the actors, I wouldn't say exactly had fun performing, but they do convey an intensity, a gravity of pleasure that is very apparent throughout the film.

8

CRIME AND DISCOURSE

ascal Kané: If you like, we could begin by talking about why you were interested in publishing the records on Pierre Rivière, and in particular your interest in seeing the case revisited today (at least in part) in a film.[1]

Michel Foucault: For me, the book was a trap. You know how much talk there is at present about delinquents and their psychology, their unconscious, instincts and desires, and so on. Psychiatrists, psychologists, and criminologists produce an endless flow of words on the phenomenon of delinquency. Yet it's a discussion that dates back nearly 150 years to the 1830s. In 1836 there was a magnificent case: a triple murder, and not only do you have all the documents from the trial of this murder, but also a truly unique testimony, that of the criminal himself, who left a memoir of more than a hundred pages. So publishing this book was a way for me of saying to all those shrinks in general—psychiatrists, psychoanalysts, psychologists—of saying to them: look, you've existed for 150 years, and here's a case contemporary with your birth. What do you have to say? Are you any better equipped to talk about it than your nineteenth-century colleagues?

Well, I can say that in a sense, I won; I won and I lost. I don't know, because of course, my secret wish was to hear criminologists, psychologists, and psychiatrists discuss the Rivière case in their usual insipid way. But they were literally reduced to silence: not one of them has spoken up and said, "This is actually what Rivière was about, I can now tell you what no one could tell you in the nineteenth century" (except one idiot, a psychoanalyst, who claimed that Rivière was the epitome of Lacanian paranoia). But with this one exception, nobody else has said a word. And it's to this extent that I think psychiatrists today have continued to share in the embarrassment of nineteenth-century psychiatrists and have shown that they have nothing more to say. But still, I must praise them for the caution and lucidity with which they have refrained from engaging in discussion on Rivière. So my gamble paid off or failed, depending on how you want to look at it.

Kané: But more generally, it's difficult to discuss the event itself, both in terms of its central focus, which is the murder, and also in terms of the figure who fomented it.

Foucault: Yes, I think Rivière's own words about his actions so overpower, or at least so thoroughly escape, all possible handles on this central core, which is the crime and the action, that what can you say that isn't an infinite step back from it all? Nonetheless, I can't see any equivalents of this phenomenon in either the history of crime or the history of discourse. It's a crime accompanied by a discourse that is so powerful and so strange that the crime eventually ends up by not existing, by vanishing, through the very fact of this discourse conducted by the person who committed the crime.

Kané: So how do you stand in relation to the impossibility of this discourse?

Foucault: Personally, I haven't said anything about Rivière's crime itself, and again, I don't think anyone can say anything about it. No, I think we should compare Rivière to Lacenaire, who was his exact contemporary, and who committed a whole series of petty, ugly, and generally failed crimes, which were not glorious at all. But Lacenaire managed through discourse, and actually very intelligent discourse, to make these crimes come to exist as true works of art and to make the criminal, that is, himself, Lacenaire, exist as a veritable artist of criminality. This was another tour de force, if you like. For decades and for more than a century he has managed to give an intense reality to actions that at the end of the day were rather ugly and vile. As a criminal he was really quite a loser, but the splendor and intelligence of his words gave substance to it all. Rivière is something else altogether: a truly extraordinary crime, reinvented by a discourse that was so much more extraordinary that the crime itself ceased to exist, and I think besides, that's what happened in the minds of his judges.

Kané: But then do you agree with Allio's project, which is more focused on the idea of a peasant voice? Or had you thought of this already?

Foucault: No, Allio is to be credited for having thought of this, but I agree with the idea entirely, as simply reconstructing the crime from the outside with actors, as if it was an event, and nothing more than a criminal event, would miss the point I think. First, the film had to be situated from within Rivière's discourse. It needed to be about the memoir and not about the crime. Second, the words of a humble Norman peasant in 1835 also needed to be situated in relation to what might have been the discourse of the peasantry at the time. What is closer to this form of discourse than the discourse that is spoken now with the same voice by peasants living in the same place? From across 150 years, you have the same voices, the same accents, the same awkward and hoarse words, which recount the same barely transposed thing. This is all due to the fact that Allio chose to commemorate this act on the same spot and almost with the same characters who existed 150 years ago. We have the same peasants who, in the same place, repeat the same action. It's a difficult feat to reduce the entire cinematic apparatus, the whole apparatus of film, to such economy, and that is truly extraordinary, quite unique, I think, in the history of film.

What's also important in Allio's film is that he allows peasants their tragedy. Basically, the tragedy for peasants up until the end of the eighteenth century was still hunger, perhaps. But, from the nineteenth century on, up until even now, perhaps, it became like any great tragedy: the tragedy of law, of law and the land. Greek tragedy is the tragedy that tells the story of the birth of law and its deadly effects on people. Rivière's case took place in 1836, that is, about twenty years after the implementation of the Civil Code. New laws were imposed on the daily lives of the peasants, and they struggled in this new legal universe. The whole Rivière drama is a drama about right, about the code, about the law and the land, marriage and property. The peasant world still revolves around this tragedy. So what's important is to mount and show this ancient drama to peasants today, a drama that is also their lives: just as Greek citizens were able to see the representation of their city in their own theater.

Kané: In your opinion, what is the role of the fact that today's Norman peasants can now remember this event and this period thanks to the film?

Foucault: You know, there's a great deal of literature on peasants, but not much peasant literature or peasant expression. But here we have a text written in 1835 by a peasant in his own language, that is, the language of a barely literate peasant. And here is the opportunity for today's peasants to play themselves, with their own resources, in this story which belonged to a generation only barely removed from the present. And, looking at the way Allio made his actors work, you probably noticed that in one way, he was very close to them, spelling things out in detail and giving them an enormous amount of support. But in another way, he gave them a lot of latitude, so that it truly was a matter of their language, their pronunciation, and their gestures. I think it's politically important, if you like, to give peasants the opportunity to perform this peasant text. Hence the importance of bringing in actors from the outside to represent the world of law: the jurists and the lawyers. These people all come down from the city and are basically exterior to this very direct communication between the nineteenth-century and twentieth-century peasants, a communication that Allio has managed to realize and, up to a certain point, has also allowed these peasant actors to realize.

Kané: But isn't there a danger that they are acquiring a voice only through such a monstrous story?

Foucault: This is indeed a concern. And Allio, when he started talking to them about the possibility of making the film, didn't quite dare tell them straight away what it was really about. But when he did tell them, he was very surprised that they accepted it really well and that the crime wasn't a problem for them. On the contrary, instead of becoming an obstacle, it became a kind of place where they could meet, talk, and share a whole lot of things from their everyday lives. In fact, instead of being an obstacle, the crime was rather liberating for them. If they had been asked to perform something closer to their daily lives and their present, they might have been more theatrical and stilted. Instead, under the cover of this distant and somewhat mythical crime, they were able to give themselves wholeheartedly to their own reality.

Kané: I was actually thinking of a rather unfortunate symmetry. It's very fashionable at present to make films about the turpitudes and the monstrosities of the bourgeoisie. Isn't there a risk here of falling into the trap of the indiscreet violence of the peasantry?

Foucault: And in the end returning to the tradition of an atrocious representation of the peasant world, as in Balzac and Zola. I don't think so. It's precisely perhaps because this violence is never present in a physical theatrical way. What you have are intensities, rumblings, things that aren't quite heard, layers, repetitions, things that are barely said, but there's no violence. There isn't that kind of lyricism of violence and peasant abjection that you seem to be concerned about. That's how it is in Allio's film, but it's also like that in the documents, in the written account. Of course, there are a few frenetic scenes—fights among the children that the parents argue about—but these scenes aren't very frequent anyway. And most important, in these scenes there is always a very, very great finesse, an acuity of feeling, subtlety even, often delicacy in the nastiness. What this means is that these characters in no way come across as those brutish beasts of unchained savagery that can be found in some of the literature on the peasantry. Everyone here is terribly clever, terribly refined, and, up to a certain point, terribly restrained.

9

THE RETURN OF PIERRE RIVIÈRE

G. *Gauthier*: As the one who discovered Pierre Rivière, did you recognize him in René Allio's film?

Michel Foucault: It wasn't really a matter of recognition. He was there, that's all. What interested me in the Rivière documents was precisely the fact that he was completely forgotten not long after his case, despite the relative notoriety of the crime. He completely disappeared from medical jurisprudence in spite of the fact that the eminent doctors of the time were interested in his case. Nobody spoke of him again: he presented a puzzle that couldn't be solved to the doctors of the time. As it happened, we were able to access all the items from the trial and, even better, Rivière's own memoir. The publication of the book relaunched the Rivière question, bringing it to the fore again after 150 years of psychiatry, after the discovery of psychoanalysis and the spread of penal medicine and criminology.[1] The book said to people today: here he is again, what do you have to say? It seems to me that Allio's film poses this same question, but with a greater urgency than the book. In this extraordinary actor, Claude Hébert, Allio found not Pierre Rivière himself but someone who was the possible launching pad for re-asking the question: who was Pierre Rivière?

Gauthier: Historical film usually has more of a tendency to provide answers than ask questions. Isn't the viewer expecting to be told who the real Pierre Rivière was instead?

Foucault: I don't think that the film claims to be true. The film doesn't claim to present the real Pierre Rivière. What's historically convincing about Allio's enterprise is not that it's reconstructing the Rivière case. The film took the documents, the memoir, what was actually pronounced by someone named Pierre Rivière, what was said by his family, by neighbors, by the judges, and asked how these words, these questions, these gestures might be put into the mouths, bodies, and attitudes of present-day people. These people were not even professional actors but peasants from the same locality, isomorphic to those involved in the 1836 case. This allows us to revive the question in a location as close as possible to the place where it was originally raised. What was important was that people from the region where the film was made were able to take part in the film, that they were able to adopt a position in relation to the different characters and events. It was important that they were able to perform this, and through their performance ask the question again.

Gauthier: Could we describe *The French Calvinists* (1972) and *I, Pierre Rivière* (1976) as a way of "doing history"? Was Allio actually doing history?

Foucault: Is Allio doing history? I don't think so. Doing history is a scholarly activity, which to a great extent is necessarily academic and takes place in universities. But what Allio is doing, and what film is able to do, is convey a sense of history. It can help us relate to history, or intensify parts of what we remember or what we've forgotten. You could look at the way Allio's films convey a sense of history, for example, how Jean Cavalier's voice in *The French Calvinists* can effectively be reactivated in the present and post-1968, and directly address the people of our time, using exactly the same words. Allio isn't showing us what happened; he isn't reactivating events, either in an imaginary way or as a meticulous reconstruction. There's a certain segment of our history that is what it is. What happens when you take this history, put its elements together, make a film, and put words into the mouths of characters?

Gauthier: There are at least two levels in Allio's two historical films: a literary level relating to manuscripts and a visual level relating to the realist pictorial tradition. Does this dual reference contribute to a better sense of history?

Foucault: These two levels would have come into conflict if the aim had been to undertake a reconstruction. But they are not in conflict insofar as Allio both invokes and conveys these elements that make up our history. In painting, in the system of representation that relates to the peasantry such as can be found in Millet, there is a certain vision that comes completely from the outside, which looks down on the peasants from on high, not in a way that deprives them of their force, but frames them in a certain way. There's that vision, which is more or less contemporary with the Rivière affair, and there's the way people such as doctors and judges encroached on the tumult and suffering of this peasant world. All this needs to be fitted together as well as partly hidden, in order to reveal the essential elements and allow the same question to be addressed. Allio's films evoke the eternal present rather than rehearsing history. It's the eternal present of what is most fleeting, that is, the everyday. This whole problem of the everyday in Allio goes from Brechtian dramaturgy right up to what he is trying to do now, which is actually very far removed from Brecht. Nonetheless, there is still a common element that is found in this strong dramatic meaning of the everyday, and its permanent presence beneath the never-ending flight of all these micro events that don't merit a mention and more or less disappear from memory. But this all actually registers at a certain level. Ultimately, every insignificant event that took place in the heart of the countryside is still in some way inscribed in the bodies of twentieth-century urban inhabitants. There is a tiny element of the peasantry, an obscure drama from the fields and the forest, the barn, that is still inscribed somewhere, has marked our bodies in a certain way, and still marks them in an infinitesimal way.

Gauthier: Do you think that someone as unique as Pierre Rivière can throw into relief the underlying forces of history, those that Brecht labeled "dark forces"?

Foucault: In one sense, Pierre Rivière managed to short-circuit and set a trap for all the mechanisms that were designed to pin him down. Rather, there was a double trap. First, he managed to escape from everything—because ultimately neither medicine nor the law knew what to do with him, and his memoir, which anticipated it all, avoided all the categorizations and potential pitfalls. When asked why he killed his little brother, he replied: "To become so detestable in the eyes of everyone, and of my father in particular, that my father wouldn't be unhappy when I was condemned to death." Second, this formidable trap he had set for everyone, which prevented him from being pinned down from the outside, brought about his conviction, and finally his death, in spite of the fact that he had been pardoned. In the face of such a wonderfully lucid project, and especially in the face of such an admirable text, certain doctors, certainly the jurors and the judges, said: "This man can't be a madman. He can't be condemned, he is so wonderfully lucid, strong and intelligent." He escaped from all the traps by bypassing all the traps, and he himself was trapped. Allio's film, through the interplay he sets up the between the text, the memoir—the voiceover—and what we see, re-creates this double trap very nicely. There is, to begin with, a kind of voice that wraps itself around everything else: the whole film takes place inside Rivière's voice. Not only is Rivière present in the film, he envelops it like a kind of thin membrane, he haunts the external boundaries of the film. Second, by bringing in the documentary voices of journalists, judges, and doctors, the film reproduces the process, which sees Rivière finally trapped by the discourse that took place around his own discourse.

Gauthier: One of your own expressions that Allio likes to use in relation to his film is "the miniscule grain of history." With such a star, isn't it true that at this late date the grain is in fact no longer miniscule?

Foucault: It's like *Blow-Up*[2] if you like, a kind of explosion that is produced in all ventures of this kind, just as in daily life. For example, when you open the newspaper and read that a man killed his wife after an argument: it's really just everyday life, which at any given moment, after an accident, a detour, a tiny excess becomes something huge and then immediately vanishes like a burst balloon. That's what the Rivière case is like, and it's that which the film shows: daily life, a dispute over a field, furniture, old clothes. That's what the unconscious of history is, not some kind of grand force or life-and-death instinct. Our historical unconscious is made up of these millions, billions of small events, which little by little, like drops of rain, erode our bodies, our way of thinking, and then by chance one of these micro events leaves traces and can become a kind of monument, a book, a film.

Gauthier: Just chance?

Foucault: Chance understood as a kind of random thing meaning that, out of all these documents, some are preserved; out of so many crimes, some come to other people's awareness;

and out of so many actions, disputes, rages, and hatreds, one of them ends in a crime. Eventually there is such a complicated tangle of reasons that the end result is a random phenomenon, meaning that 150 years later, a film comes to be made about the day-to-day conflicts in this Rivière family, a film that will be seen by tens of thousands of people. I am really fascinated by this kind of vagary.

Gauthier: Nonetheless, we are only too happy to believe that there is a certain intelligence to history, that it doesn't make its selections at random.

Foucault: We can of course analyze why, at a particular moment, people have become interested in this type of crime, why the problems of madness and crime have become prominent concerns in our culture, and why a peasant tragedy has an impact on us. All the same, this particular accident lends an aesthetic poignancy to these events. Problems like these occurred in their thousands at the time. Why did this one lead to murder, why did this murder make such an impact at the time, why was it then not just forgotten but completely forgotten? How was it that a dust-loving individual such as myself came across this text one day? Actually, I can tell you how I came across this text. I was systematically sorting through all the medico-legal appraisals of criminal acts from the first half of the nineteenth century. I expected to find a few dozen documents, but instead I came across hundreds. Overwhelmed by this pile of papers, I simply took the biggest. And then it wasn't just a medical certificate I stumbled across, it was this extraordinary language, which didn't belong to a doctor. I read it later that evening, of course, and I was amazed. If it hadn't been me, it would have been someone else perhaps, as an interest is starting to emerge in these kinds of stories, but as you can see, a series of wonderful coincidences has occurred. The story would definitely not have had such an impact if it hadn't been for one of the doctors on the scene, Vastel, who had a student-teacher relationship with prominent psychiatrists in Paris. It really was a matter of a series of small things like that. Broadly speaking, there's an intelligibility to all this, but the trajectory of events from Pierre Rivière, his mother, and his father right down to us is made up of a certain number of chance occurrences that lend to Rivière's return a great deal of dramatic intensity.

Gauthier: Allio often draws a contrast between small history and big history: that is, between everyday life and exceptional events. But by focusing on small history, one gains the impression that it is, in fact, big history that is being made. At the end of the day, Pierre Rivière is more important now than many of his formerly illustrious contemporaries from 1836.

Foucault: Of course. This is one of the interesting things that's happening at the moment. One of the most successful history books in recent months has been Le Roy Ladurie's book on Montaillou.[3] The figures from this history now have a presence in French historiography that is almost as strong as Mirabeau or La Fayette. We are now interested in the everyday. But historians have actually been interested in the everyday for a long time, from the history of sensibility and feelings to the history of material culture affecting the organization of everyday life. But this interest has been in relatively general terms. In recent years, monographs have unearthed the most anonymous people from this general area of everyday life, from housing conditions to parent-child relationships. The individual has become a sort of historical figure. This is new, and Allio's film is absolutely in keeping with this trend.

Gauthier: One remark that has often been made about Allio is that he's interested in characters who are going through a process of change, and this is quite clear in relation to Pierre Rivière. Can you also see evidence of historical change, a period in the process of transformation in the film?

Foucault: In Rivière's time, the peasantry, which had been framed by old and very outdated forms of feudalism, was dealing with the appearance of a new system of law after 1789 and after the empire. The Civil Code was beginning to make an impact on rural areas, bringing with it a very new relation to property, to judicial bodies, and to the law. It was a relation that was at once awkward—people were not familiar with the texts—and also very avid and intense, since, after all, what was at issue in all these debates was fortune, wealth, property—the basic conditions of life. It was a problem concerning law, in short. When we remember that all classical tragedies are tragedies concerning the law (Greek tragedies are always dramas about the law), you could say that what we have here, at least in its beginnings at the very basic level of an extremely petty rural drama, is a relation that has all the intensity of the tragic: the relation between the law and the people.

Gauthier: Isn't it also a period when the relations of control and surveillance that you have outlined elsewhere were put into place?

Foucault: Yes indeed. But in the Rivière case, you don't feel this directly. Those systems of surveillance that were guaranteed by the police, the judiciary, medicine, and so on—which at the same time also functioned as systems of analysis and understanding, rendering people and their behavior intelligible—had not yet penetrated into the countryside. Far from it. This makes the situation very difficult to analyze. It's really interesting to see how the examining magistrate asks the questions in the film, and how people respond: sometimes completely off on a tangent, sometimes doing no more than repeating the judge's question. They don't know how to play the role that they have been since taught to play, which is to make a certain number of psychological judgments concerning the criminal.

Gauthier: Isn't there a change of register when Rivière roams the countryside?

Foucault: What I really like about the film's construction is that this vagrancy is placed at the end, after the conviction. The film has a false ending, and after Rivière is convicted the film begins again with the vagrancy that preceded his arrest. The film thus introduces a dimension that allows Rivière not to be caught in the medico-judicial trap that condemns him. He leaves, he flees, he escapes from all this and becomes this floating figure existing outside justice, beyond crime, outside society, a figure who is at the same time both running away and in suspense. This looks like an error in the film's construction, but in fact it allows Rivière to break out of history, to break away from reality.

Gauthier: For all its reputation for being concrete, is film actually better at evoking dreamlike wandering than at doing history?

Foucault: You can't expect film to answer the question of knowledge; you would be on losing ground there. You can ask other questions, however. Film allows you to have a relation to history, to establish a mode of historical presence, a sense of history that is very different from what you can achieve through writing. Let's take Moatti's series *Le pain noir*.[4] Its success and importance depended on the fact that, far more so than a novel, it was related to a history that everybody had some memory of, namely, our grandmothers' lives. Our grandmothers lived that history. It's not at the level of what we know but at the level of our bodies, the way we act, the way we do things, think, and dream, and abruptly those mysterious little pebbles inside us become unstuck.

They found an old lady of eighty-five in a little town in Normandy, who was born in the very village where the crime was committed, and who remembered being threatened with Pierre

Rivière as a child. This was after the publication of the book, so I wasn't able to include her. There was a kind of direct continuity there, and she really had heard it spoken about. For others, it was a matter of another kind of memory, but it still existed.

Gauthier: Isn't Pierre Rivière still a film based on a book, or rather that takes a detour via a book to get to the sources?

Foucault: On the contrary, what strikes me is that it's not a film based on a book, it's something else. Of course the film made use of documents from the book, but the documents were made for this. In the book we wanted to raise the question of Rivière again and collect everything that had been said about Rivière at the time and after. The song, for example, came after. Generally, when a crime was committed, pamphlet publishers hastily reprinted stories relating to another crime. Songs were sung to begin with, but these songs developed into no more than a somewhat empty form in the nineteenth century and also a justification for the publication of these pamphlets. The government also took a rather a dim view of these pamphlets, as political tracts were slipped into them. So they made up for it by inserting a moral at the end, a bit like the tabloids. In compiling all this, we were, after all, producing a scholarly book and a book that we were addressing to psychiatrists, psychoanalysts, and all those interested in these kinds of issues. But in France at least, no one at all took up the kind of challenge that Pierre Rivière's case posed. There was a total, all-round silence, which proves at least their awareness of their limits. In contrast to this, there was a boom in film and theater.

Gauthier: Your work was a scholarly undertaking, but the real audience was the artistic world. Why do you think that is?

Foucault: This kind of great divide between knowledge and art is in the process of breaking down anyway. There has been a great deal of discussion about knowledge being discredited, but

I'd say that just the opposite is happening, namely, that knowledge is being reappraised. What's happening is simply that certain calcified and boring forms of knowledge are being discredited because there's currently a veritable thirst for knowledge. So I'm not surprised that a scholarly book has circulated in this manner; the institutional holders of knowledge have been asked many questions to which they have been unable to respond, in spite of the fact that they involve and affect many people. The general relationship that people have at present to, say, madness is extremely important, even in the scholarly arena. Underlying psychiatric knowledge of mental illness since 1830, there has been a kind of perception of madness that has constantly supported and fed into it. This relationship to madness started changing for people about fifteen years ago, even before it began to change for a certain number of psychiatrists, and all this for reasons that science has little to do with. In any case, it is certain that the scientific discourse on madness can no longer remain the same, and to that extent, even if psychiatrists never pick up the Rivière case, the fact that it has had such a strong impact will mean that doctors will have to take it into account. Of course, they are already taking it into account, without being aware of it, when they are faced with someone who has committed a crime. The Rivière enigma is by no means a lost cause, but the fact that it remains an enigma is not in vain, or without effects.

Gauthier: Do you feel a certain uneasiness every time Rivière is brought back to life in film or theater?

Foucault: I and the other people who worked on this case set a rule for ourselves: the text didn't belong to us, the work we did on it was both a pleasure and also a kind of obscure duty, but we weren't going to interfere with the way the documents were used. When Allio came to speak to me I was really happy, as in my opinion, Allio had done one of the best things in recent years in terms of treatments of history and film with his film *The French Calvinists*. Now that the film is finished, I am somewhat hesitant to talk about it, as I don't think I can really see it properly. I've tried, but I still see it through the book and through the documents. I have a completely skewed perception. I also witnessed the work that went into developing the film. This is the first time I've seen a film so close up, so it was a real initiation for me. I now see the resulting film through the production as well as through the book, and my perception is a little feverish. Not that I doubt the quality of the film, but I so intensely wanted to put myself in the place of someone who hadn't read the book, even just for a few moments, in the place of someone who knew nothing about the history, and who suddenly heard these strange voices, these actors who are not actors.

10

THE DULL REGIME OF TOLERANCE

Where do children come from? From storks, a flower, the Good Lord, the Calabrian uncle. But have a look at the faces of these kids: they certainly don't give the impression that they believe what they're saying. The answers to these adult questions, delivered with smiles, silences, a distant tone, and shifty glances, display a perfidious docility; they hold on to the right to keep things private that they would rather whisper. The stork is a way of making fun of adults, giving them a run for their money. Eager for the questions not to go any further, this is the ironic sign that adults are intrusive, that they need to be kept out of the picture, so that children can continue to tell their own tales to each other about what has been left out.

So begins Pasolini's film.

"An inquiry into sexuality" is a very strange translation of *Comizi d'amore* (*Love Meetings*, 1964): a fair, meeting, or perhaps forum of love. This is the ancient game of "the symposium" but played out in the open, on beaches and bridges, on street corners, with children playing ball, loitering boys, bored bathers, prostitutes in clusters on a boulevard, and factory workers after hours. At a far remove from the confessional, and also far from an inquiry where questions are asked about the most secret things with a guarantee of confidentiality, this is instead *The Word on the Street About Love*. The street is, after all, the most spontaneous form of Mediterranean conviviality.

Pasolini holds out his microphone almost in passing to strolling and meandering groups, asking a general question about "love," about that ambiguous area where sex, the couple, pleasure, the family, engagement and its customs, prostitution and its charges all intersect. Someone makes up their mind and answers somewhat hesitantly and then, gaining in confidence, speaks on behalf of the others. They gather around, approving or grumbling, arms on shoulders, face against face, laughter, affection, a slight feverishness circulating quickly among the bodies that crowd and brush against each other. The more restraint and distance they use to speak about themselves, the more their contact is warm and lively. Adults stand side by side and hold forth, young people speak briefly and hug each other. Pasolini the interviewer fades away: Pasolini the film-maker watches with all ears.

The document is invaluable if you are more interested in the mystery of what is not being said than in what is actually being said. After the long reign of what has been (too hastily) described as Christian morality, one might have expected a ferment of sexuality in this Italy of the early sixties. Not in the least. The answers are obstinately couched in terms of the law: for or against divorce, for or against the husband's preeminence, for or against compulsory virginity for girls, for or against the condemnation of homosexuals. It's as if Italian society at the time, caught between the secrets of penance and the prescriptions of the law, had not yet found a voice for those public confidences on sex that the media broadcast today.

"They aren't talking? It's because they are afraid," explains Musatti, a humdrum psychoanalyst, whom Pasolini brings in from time to time, along with Moravia, to comment on the investigation in progress. But Pasolini obviously doesn't believe that for a minute. It's not, I think, an obsessive fear of sex that runs through the film but a kind of historical apprehension, a prescient and confused hesitancy in the face of a new regime that was starting to form in Italy at the time: a regime of tolerance. And it is there that the divisions become clear, among this crowd who, when asked about love, share their views on the law instead. Do we see divisions between men and women, peasants and city dwellers, rich and poor? Yes, of course, but most of all between young people and the others. The latter are afraid of a regime that will upset all the painful and subtle adjustments that the reigning ecosystem of sex had held in place (with the prohibition of divorce placing unequal restraints on men and women, with the brothel serving as a complementary figure to the family, with the price of virginity and the cost of marriage). Young people approach this change in quite a different way: not with cries of joy, but with a mixture of seriousness and distrust, because they know it's tied to economic changes that are very likely to bring back inequalities in age, wealth, and status. Basically, the dull mornings of tolerance don't appeal to anybody, and no one is in a hurry to celebrate sex. Resigned or angry, the old worry: what will happen to *the* law? And "young people" reply obstinately: what will happen to rights, *our* rights?

This film, which is now fifteen years old, can serve as a benchmark. Made a year after *Mamma Roma* (1962), Pasolini was pursuing what was to become the grand saga of youth in his work. He didn't see the "adolescents" of psychologists in these young people but rather the contemporary form of "youth" that, since the Middle Ages, since Rome and Greece, our societies have been unable to integrate. It's a form they feared or rejected but never managed to subdue, except to have young people killed in war from time to time.

Anyway, 1963 marked Italy's brash entry into this movement of expansion-consumption-tolerance that Pasolini took stock of ten years later, in his *Écrits corsaires*.[1] The violence of the book responds to the unease of the film.

The year 1963 was also one that saw the beginning of a challenge to multiple forms of power all over Europe and in the United States, challenges the pundits tell us are "fashionable." Well, good! This "fashion" might be around for some time to come, just as it was in those days in Bologna.

11

THE FOUR HORSEMEN
OF THE APOCALYPSE

ans-Jürgen Syberberg's film Hitler: A Film from Germany *(1977), was quite badly received in West Germany and the United States in terms of its aesthetic approach, as it was judged too indulgent. This interview with theater director Bernard Sobel is part of a series of articles in which Susan Sontag, Heiner Müller, Douglas Sirk, and Francis Coppola all defended the film. Foucault was familiar with Syberberg's complete filmography.*

Bernard Sobel: When I saw the film for the first time in Germany, I was spellbound and bewitched. I was affected because I have some familiarity with Germany and its culture. And I was disturbed. I thought there was something perverse about this film. In fact, everyone is a little wary of this film. What was your reaction? Did you say "this is what should have been done!"?

Michel Foucault: No, because there is no *one* thing that should have been done about what happened between 1930 and 1945; there were a thousand, ten thousand, an infinite number of things that should have been done. It's certainly true that the wall of silence that has been erected around Nazism since 1945 for political reasons is such that one cannot help but ask the question: "What has this become in the minds of Germans?

What has this become in their hearts? What has this become in their bodies?" It was bound to become something, and there has been a somewhat anxious wait to see how all this was going to come out at the other end of the tunnel. What myth, what story, what wounds were going to appear? Syberberg's film is a beautiful monster. I say "beautiful" because this is what struck me the most, and this is perhaps what you mean when you talk about the perverse character of this film. I'm not talking about the aesthetics of film here, which is something I know nothing about. He has managed to bring out a certain beauty in this history without concealing what was sordid, ignoble, and mundanely abject about it. It is here, perhaps, where he has grasped Nazism at its most seductive, a certain intensity of abjection, a certain sparkle of mediocrity, which was doubtless one of Nazism's powers of enchantment.

Sobel: When I saw the film, I also had a strange feeling: I had the amazing revelation that young people experienced Nazism as a utopia, as a real utopia. I thought it was very significant that Syberberg doesn't judge and doesn't condemn but rather makes you aware of the fact that a "normally constituted" man, according to conventional standards, could have been a Nazi.

Foucault: Simone Veil said about the film on Eva Braun that was broadcast a few days ago on television that "it banalized the horror."[1] This is quite true, and the film on Eva Braun, which was a French film, was positively stupefying in this regard. But Syberberg's film does the opposite: it makes the mundane vile. It unearths the potential for ignominy in the banality of a certain way of thinking, of a certain way of life, and of a certain number of ordinary European daydreams in the 1930s. In this respect, this film is the exact opposite of the films that Simone Veil so rightly condemned. One day I would love to see the film on Eva Braun interspersed with different scenes from

Syberberg's film. The former seems to have been made from the old-fashioned, boring, genteel, and proper postcards sent by a respectable middle-class European family on holidays during the 1930s. The value of Syberberg's film is precisely in showing that horror is banal, that banality contains dimensions of horror within itself, that horror and banality are reversible. In tragedy and philosophy the problem is what status you give to the four horsemen of the Apocalypse. Are they lavish dark heroes who await the end of the world to burst onto the scene? What form will they take when they suddenly appear, and what countenance will they display? Plague, the great massacres of war, famine? Or are they four little worms that we all have in our heads, at the back of our mind, deep within our hearts?

I believe this is where the strength of Syberberg's film lies. It successfully draws attention to those moments when what was happening in Europe between 1930 and 1945 did indeed evoke the great dark horsemen of the Apocalypse, but at the same time it shows the kind of symbiotic relationship between the four riders and those ordinary little worms.

12

WERNER SCHROETER AND MICHEL
FOUCAULT IN CONVERSATION

T*he editors of* Dits et écrits *note the following: "When Werner Schroeter's* The Death of Maria Malibran *was released in 1972, Foucault wrote a text ("The Nondisciplinary Camera Versus Sade") that the filmmaker saw as the fairest and most accurate analysis of his work of the period. Foucault and Schroeter didn't know each other. They met for the first time in December 1981."*[1]

Michel Foucault: What struck me when I saw *The Death of Maria Malibran* (1972) and *Willow Springs* (1973) was that these films were not about love but about passion.

Werner Schroeter: The central idea of *Willow Springs* rests on an obsessional dependency linking four characters, none of whom knows the exact reasons for this dependency. For example, Ila von Hasperg, who plays the role of the servant and housekeeper, doesn't know why she is a victim of this relationship of dependency with Magdalena. I see it as an obsession.

Foucault: I think that we're talking about pretty much the same thing. To begin with, you can't really say that these women love each other. There's no love in *Maria Malibran*. What is passion? It's a state; it's something that just happens to you, takes hold of you, and seizes you by both shoulders. It doesn't stop and doesn't begin anywhere. In fact, you have no idea where it's coming from. Passion turns up just like that. It's a constantly mobile state, but it doesn't move to a given point. There are high points and low points and times where it becomes white hot. It drifts. It sways. It's a kind of unstable moment that keeps going for obscure reasons, perhaps through inertia. Ultimately, it tries both to hold firm and to disappear. Passion creates all the conditions necessary for it to continue and yet at the same time it destroys itself. In a state of passion you're not blind. It's simply that in these situations of passion, you are not yourself. Being yourself no longer makes sense. You see things very differently.

In passion, there is also a quality of pain-pleasure that is very different from what can be found in desire or in so-called sadism or masochism. I don't see a sadistic or masochistic relationship between these women, but what does exist is a completely inseparable state of pain-pleasure. These are not two qualities that are mixed together; they are one and the same. Each woman suffers greatly, but you can't say that they make each other suffer. We see three types of ongoing suffering that are at the same time entirely chosen, because there is no need for this suffering to be there and present.

These women are chained in a state of suffering that binds them together, which they are unable to break away from but which at the same time they would do anything to free themselves from. All of this is different from love. In love there is, in a way, someone who is in charge of this love, whereas passion circulates between the partners.

Schroeter: Love is less active than passion.

Foucault: The state of passion is a mixed state between different partners.

Schroeter: Love is a state of grace, of distance. A few days ago, during a discussion, Ingrid Caven said that love was a selfish emotion because it has nothing to do with the partner.

Foucault: It's perfectly possible to love without being loved in return. It's a solitary affair. That's why, in a sense, love is always full of solicitations toward the other. That's its weakness, because it's always asking for something from the other, whereas a state of passion between two or three people is something that allows intense communication.

Schroeter: This means that passion contains a great communicative strength within itself, whereas love is an isolated state. I find it really depressing knowing that love is an internal creation and invention.

Foucault: Love can become passion, that is, the kind of state we've been talking about.

Schroeter: And hence suffering.

Foucault: This state of mutual and reciprocal suffering truly is communication. It seems to me that this is what's happening between these women. Their faces and bodies are not lit by desire but by passion.

Schroeter: In a debate a few years ago, someone told me that *Willow Springs* was like Albert Camus's *Cross Purpose*.[2]

Foucault: In fact, I thought your film had come from Camus's book. It's the old story of the Red Inn found in many stories in European literature. It's the story of an inn run by women who kill travelers venturing into their "domain." Camus used this in his novel.

Schroeter: I wasn't aware of this story when I directed *Willow Springs*. Later, after I read Camus's book, I realized that what mattered in the story was the mother/son relationship. The inn was run by the mother and sister who were waiting for the son. When the son returned, the mother and sister murdered him because they didn't recognize him.

Willow Springs was sparked off by Christine Kaufmann, who had just been working with me on my production of Gotthold Ephraim Lessing's *Emilia Galotti*. One day, her ex-husband

Tony Curtis came and took their two children, who had been in her custody for five years. We didn't have the money to fight this feckless father. At the time, I had proposed a low-budget film to German television titled *The Death of Marilyn Monroe*. I left for America with Christine Kaufmann, Magdalena Montezuma, and Ila von Hasperg, because Christine and I had the idea getting of the two children back. It was the first time I'd been to Los Angeles and California. The idea of *Willow Springs* came up while I was seeing the lawyers and exploring the area. In Germany, some people saw in it a critique of the homosexual reign of terror. Finally, we ended up in the same situation as the film's protagonists. We were completely cut off in a small hotel ten kilometers from Willow Springs.

Foucault: How do these three women end up living together?

Schroeter: What I want to say first is that we were already together. *Willow Springs* is a reflection of the situation we were living in and what I felt with these three women, considering that I had been working with Magdalena, Ila, and Christine for several years. Ila always poetically foregrounded her ugliness, Christine was icily beautiful and very friendly, and the third, Magdalena, was very depressive and very domineering. This situation built up in a very unfavorable political space, in a spot inhabited by fascists. The town was run by an American Nazi. It was a terrifying place.

Do you have a leaning toward passion or toward love?

Foucault: Passion.

Schroeter: The conflict between love and passion is the subject of all my plays in the theater. Love is a spent force that is destined to be lost immediately because it's never reciprocal. It's always suffering and total nihilism, like life and death. The authors I like are all suicidal, for example, Kleist and Hölderlin—who is someone I think I understand, but outside the literary context.

From childhood I've known that I had to work, not because I was told that it was necessary—I was much too anarchist and too turbulent to believe that—but because I knew that given there were so few opportunities to communicate in life, you needed to take advantage of work in order to express yourself. In fact, to work is to create. I once knew a very creative whore who took a creative and artistic social approach to her clientele. That's my dream. When I don't achieve these states of passion, I work.

What's your life like?

Foucault: Very sedate.

Schroeter: Can you tell me about your passion?

Foucault: For eighteen years I have been living in a state of passion with someone, for someone. Perhaps at some point this passion turned to love. Actually, it's a state of shared passion, an ongoing state, which has no other reason to end other than itself, which totally inhabits me, and in which I'm fully invested. I don't think there's a single thing in the world, absolutely nothing, that would stop me from going to him, talking to him.

Schroeter: What differences have you noticed in the state of passion as lived by a woman and as lived by a man?

Foucault: In these nontransparent states of communication that are passion, I would tend to say that it's not possible to know whether passion is stronger among homosexuals, when you don't know what the other's pleasure is, what the other is, and what's happening with the other.

Schroeter: The object of my passion is in Italy. It's a passion that can't be defined in exclusively sexual terms. He's a boy who has his male friends and his female lovers. He's someone who also has a passion for me, I think. That would be so good if it was true! I've said since I was a boy that for me, it's an advantage being homosexual, because it's wonderful.

Foucault: We have objective proof that homosexuality is more interesting than heterosexuality: namely, that there are a considerable number of heterosexuals who would like to become homosexuals but very few homosexuals who really want to become heterosexual. It's like going from East to West Germany. We can love a woman, have an intense relationship with a woman, more so perhaps than with a boy, but we would never want to become a heterosexual.

Schroeter: My really good friend Rosa von Pranheim, who has made many films on the subject of homosexuality, said to me one day: "You're an insufferable coward," because I refused to sign a petition against the repression of homosexuals. At the time, a press campaign launched by the magazine *Der Stern* was saying homosexuals ought to "come out." I replied to her: "I'd like to sign your petition, but I can't sign anything against the repression of homosexuals, because if there's one thing I've never suffered from in my life, it is my homosexuality." I was already much loved by women, but they were even more attentive once they knew I was homosexual.

Maybe I filmed *Willow Springs* out of guilt, as I've done a lot of film and theater with women. I can see the difference in my passion for a woman like Magdalena Montezuma, with whom I share a deep lifelong friendship, and my passion for my Italian friend. Perhaps psychologically—and I emphasize that I know nothing about psychology—it's a matter of anxiety in relation to men and guilt in relation to women. My motivation is very strange. I can't define it. In Prague, for my film *Day of the Idiots* (1981), I worked with thirty women, all of whom I've worked with for the past thirteen years.

Foucault: You can't say why?

Schroeter: No.

Foucault: One of the most striking things about your film is that we know nothing about what's happening between these women, about the nature of these little worlds. And yet, at the same time, there's a kind of clarity and straightforwardness.

Schroeter: I can't define the cause of my feelings. For example, seeing my Italian friend sends me into a state of passion.

Foucault: I'm going to take an example. When I see a film by Bergman, who is also a filmmaker obsessed with women and by love between women, I'm bored. Bergman bores me, because I think he wants to try to see what is going on between these women. Whereas with you, there's a kind of immediacy that doesn't try to show what's happening, and which means the question is not even raised. And your way of completely avoiding the psychological film seems fruitful to me. Instead, we see bodies, faces, lips and eyes. You let them perform a kind of evidence of passion.

Schroeter: Psychology doesn't interest me. I don't believe in it.

Foucault: We should get back to what you were saying earlier about creativity. You've lost it, in life, in what you're writing and in the film you're making, precisely at that moment where you want to start investigating the nature of something's identity. It's at that point that you've "missed" it, because you've started classifying things. The problem exactly is to create something that happens between ideas and to make it impossible to give it a name. So at every instant, the aim is to try to provide a coloration, a shape, and an intensity to something that never says what it is. It's precisely that, which is the art of living. The art of living means killing psychology, and creating unnameable individualities, beings, relationships, and qualities within oneself and with others. If you can't manage to do this in your life, it doesn't deserve to be lived. I make no distinction between those who make their lives a work of art and those who create artistic work during their lives. A life can be a perfect and sublime work: this was something the Greeks knew but we have completely forgotten, especially since the Renaissance.

Schroeter: This is the system of psychological terror. Film consists only of psychological dramas and psychological thrillers.

I'm not afraid of death. It might be arrogant to say this, but it's the truth. Ten years ago, I was afraid of death. To look death in the face is a dangerous anarchist sentiment according to the establishment. Society plays on terror and fear.

Foucault: Something that has preoccupied me for a while now is the realization of how difficult it is to commit suicide. Let's consider and list the limited number of means of suicide that we have at our disposal, each more disgusting than the last: gas, which is dangerous for the neighbors; hanging, which is unpleasant for the cleaner who discovers the body the next morning; and jumping out the window, which creates a mess on the pavement. In addition to this, suicide is still considered very negatively by society. Not only are we told that it's not right to commit suicide, but there's a belief that if someone does commit suicide, then things were going very badly for them.

Schroeter: What you are saying is strange, because I just had a discussion with my friend Alberte Barsacq, the costume designer for my films and plays, about two friends who committed suicide recently. I don't understand how somebody who is very depressed could have the strength to commit suicide. I could only kill myself in a state of grace or in a state of extreme pleasure, but certainly not in a state of depression.

Gérard Courant: One thing that really surprised some people about Jean Eustache's suicide is that in the days before his suicide he was feeling better.[3]

Foucault: I'm sure that Jean Eustache committed suicide when he was in fine form. People don't understand because he was feeling well. Actually, this is something that no one wants to admit. I'm in favor of a genuine cultural struggle to get people to relearn that there is no conduct that is finer than suicide and, as a consequence, needs to be thought through with as much attention. You should work on your suicide your whole life.

Schroeter: Do you know Améry, the German writer, who some years ago wrote a book on suicide and who proposed some of the same ideas as yourself? He later committed suicide.

We live in a system that operates on guilt. Look at illness. I've lived in Africa and India, where people are not in the least embarrassed about being open about their condition to the rest of society. Even lepers are able to put themselves on show. In Western society, as soon as you are sick, you need to be afraid, to hide, and you can no longer live a normal life. It's ridiculous that illness is not a part of life. I have a completely schizoid relationship with psychology. Picking up my lighter and a cigarette is no big deal. The important thing is performing the action. This is what gives me my dignity. Knowing that my mother smoked too much when I was five years old doesn't interest me in terms of the knowledge of my own personality.

Foucault: This is one of the most fundamental choices we now have in Western societies. We've been taught throughout the twentieth century that there's nothing you can do if you don't know anything about yourself. The truth about yourself is a condition of existence, but you can easily imagine societies where no attempt is made to address the issue of what you are and where it makes no sense. These are societies where the important thing is the art of putting existence to work in order to do what we do, to be what we are: an art of the self that is the complete opposite of the self. Making one's being an object of art, now that's worth the effort.

Schroeter: I remember a sentence from your book *The Order of Things*, which I really liked: "If those arrangements were to disappear . . . then one can certainly wager that man would be erased, like a face drawn in sand at the edge of the sea."[4] I have never been angry with anyone. I don't understand how the bourgeois system of psychology, which continues to play one individual off against another, can continue to be tolerated. I can very well argue with someone and then the next day resume normal relations with them. (I'm not talking about a relationship of love or passion.) Every day I am another. Psychology is a mystery to me. Freud has built a very dangerous system for us that is used by every Western society and goes right over our heads.

I would like to cite an example of an action that to me appears quite anodyne but would be misinterpreted in the Freudian context.

When I returned from America after the filming of *Willow Springs*, I was very tired, and my mother wanted to wash me, because she likes doing this. At one point, I started to pee in the bath. Imagine the situation: a mother of sixty and her son of twenty-seven. I laughed a lot. In any case, I always pee in the bath. Why not pee? What else can you say? It's a fraternal relationship, which has nothing to do with incest, because I have never had an imaginary erotic relationship with my mother. I see her as a friend. I don't see any problem there unless I reduce this action to a bourgeois psychological context.

Novalis wrote a poem that I love: *Hymns to the Night*. He explains why he prefers night to day. That's German romanticism.

When I put on *Lohengrin* three years ago in Kassel, I was asked what the idea was behind my production. My only response was that the music of *Lohengrin* is extremely beautiful and that it's romantic music that you can overdo, given Wagner already had an awareness of the industrial age. I specified that I wouldn't give them the pleasure of playing the little devil and denouncing Wagner's music and work. I found that it was so overloaded with multiple interpretations, especially ideological ones, that I decided to offer a fairly childish interpretation with very primitive staging like puppet theater. The sky was studded with a thousand illuminated stars above a golden pyramid and glittering costumes. I worked almost exclusively with the conductor to make the music as beautiful as possible. My Berlin friends on the far left asked how I could do Wagner this way. I told them that I refused to do what Patrice Chéreau did with his use of evening gowns and industrial machinery in *The Ring of the Nibelung* so as to denounce Wagner, making him a precursor of the Third Reich.

Foucault: I don't think that was what Chéreau was intending to do.[5] What I thought was good about Chéreau's approach was that his creation of an industrial vision didn't necessarily mean that he was denouncing something. Saying that there are elements of that reality present in Wagner is not a simplistic and denunciative critique, of the kind: "Look at Wagner's reality: it's the reality of bourgeois society."

Schroeter: I always work with the surroundings. Kassel's theater, where I did the production, has a good musical ambience. I organized my production essentially around the actors and singers. If I had an enormous singer in the cast, like the one who played Elsa, I didn't try to camouflage her with a black outline and white clothing. I designed the production so that when Elsa is accused in the first act of murdering Gottfried and she recounts her visions, I showed them as collective visions, as if Elsa, with her visions, was part of an amorous and passionate collective. At the end, when Lohengrin reveals himself to be a man, we realize that he's a real person and not a collective vision. At that moment, Elsa commits suicide and Ortrud, who represents the old culture, triumphs. For me, it is Ortrud who is the positive and passionate woman in the work.

This is music that needs to be "attacked" naïvely. I really love the way Boulez conducts Wagner, but I don't see Wagner's music that way at all.

Performers are really ashamed of not being able to live up to his genius, and in the end they don't live up to anything. Wagner was like anyone else, but with a lot of talent and a great idea of course. You shouldn't start with respect. You need to respect the quality of the work but not the genius behind it. The music of *Lohengrin* is very musical, like Viennese music. That's what I tried to show in my production because I don't like luxury or Bayreuth.

Foucault: When you directed *The Death of Maria Malibran*, did you think of the music first?

Schroeter: More than anything else I was thinking of suicide: I was thinking of the people I loved and of those whom I felt a passion for, such as Maria Callas, with whom I have always been very much in love. *The Death of Maria Malibran* also came about through reading a Spanish book on Maria Malibran, reading a text on the death of Janis Joplin and another on the death of Jimi Hendrix, all people I admired enormously.

Maria Callas was my childhood erotic fantasy. In my fourteen-year-old erotic dreams, I imagined her peeing with me watching her. This was always something that had nothing to do with Maria Callas's actual image and the respect and friendship that I felt for her. She was *the* erotic woman par excellence. Maria Callas was a total passion for me. Strangely, she never frightened me. I remember a discussion I had with her in Paris, in 1976, when she told me she only knew people who were afraid of her. I said to her: "How can anyone possibly be afraid of you?" She was exceptionally nice, a little Greek-American girl. She was the same at fifty. I suggested: "Do you want an article published in *France-soir*: 'Maria Callas is looking for a man?'" She laughed a lot. "You'll see, a hundred people will turn up." People were so afraid of her that they didn't dare to come and see her. She lived a very solitary life, which was a pity, because apart from her genius, she was fabulously nice and kind.

There's one thing that fascinates me that I find quite unimaginable! I have been working with the same ten people or so for the past twelve years, but members of this group have shown virtually no interest in each other. Magdalena Montezuma and Christine Kaufmann have no profound interest in each other, neither do Christine and Ingrid Caven, and so on. Magdalena and Ingrid, who like and admire each other a great deal, do have a vital interest in each other, but this is the exception. If the director isn't there, there's no vital communication between them.

APPENDIX
FOUCAULT AT THE MOVIES—
A PROGRAM OF FILMS

This book was originally accompanied by a program of films that was shown at the Villa Arson in Nice from February to June 2011. The films shown included a number of those discussed by Foucault, films referred to in the present book, as well as a selection of other films that engaged with history and recent political events in various ways. The program took place on February 11–14, March 20–22, and April 10–25 and was held as part of a series titled "The Cinema of Thought" under the auspices of L'ÉCLAT (Lieu d'Expériences pour le Cinéma, les Lettres, Arts et Technologies). An extract from the introduction to the program and the list of films is included here.[1]

INTRODUCTION TO THE PROGRAM (EXTRACT)

Patrice Maniglier and Dork Zabunyan

Can film allow history to be written differently? Can it seize upon and show those tiny elements that constitute the cogs of what Foucault called a "technology of power" in all their unexpected and rigorous arrangements? Can film contribute to a critique of our present that exposes the logics that other modes of representation miss? This series aims, among other things, to show films that exploit the micropolitical potential of film. More generally, the intention is to focus on the problematics of the relationship between film and history. This relationship will be explored by philosophers and historians as well as by those engaged in film studies (critics, film theorists, and specialists in all kinds of images including documentaries, animation, new media, and so on).

In other words, it's about considering what film can bring to all those today, who in one way or another adopt the archaeological approach that Foucault followed in his own era, while at the same time examining the problems that this approach opens up for those who question the cinematographic image and its components, evolution, and mutations. For example, how can the concept of the archive be used within the framework of film analysis? What can be made of the history of film as an object of study when it is approached with the tools used by the author of *The Birth of the Clinic*? What encounters can we see between Foucauldian descriptions of the analysis of disciplinary powers and methods of describing the moving image (and its transformations)? Further, how can the critique of the "retro" fashion in film during the 1970s encourage the reactivation today of questions about the reconstruction of history in film, beyond the facilities of a thematic approach?

FILM PROGRAM, FEBRUARY 11–14, 2011

Videograms of a Revolution, compiled by Harun Farocki and Andrei Ujica (Germany, 1992)

A documentary put together from over 125 hours of news broadcasts and amateur footage of the Romanian Revolution of 1989.

The Lady and the Duke, directed by Eric Rohmer (France, 2001)

A film based on the memoirs of the Scottish royalist aristocrat Grace Elliott in the aftermath of the French Revolution.

Ivan the Terrible, directed by Sergei M. Eisenstein (USSR, 1945)

Commissioned and then rejected by Stalin, Eisenstein's masterpiece on the betrayals, intrigues, and abuses of power during the reign of Ivan the Terrible in sixteenth-century Russia.

Jeanne la pucelle: Les batailles, directed by Jacques Rivière (France, 1994)

A film that deals with Joan of Arc's earlier life and her first battle, with an emphasis on her warrior persona.

Détruire, dit-elle, directed by Marguerite Duras (France, 1969)

The complex interactions of four characters in a secluded hotel in a forest.

Redacted, directed by Brian de Palma (USA, 2007)

A story based on a shocking event during the Iraq War in 2006, from multiple points of view involving American soldiers, the media, and the local Iraqi community.

Lili Marleen, directed by Rainer W. Fassbinder (West Germany, 1981)

Set during World War II, a film about the romance between a German singer and a Swiss Jewish composer.

Michel Foucault par lui-même, directed by Philippe Calderon (France, 2003)

A documentary on Foucault.

FILM PROGRAM, MARCH 20–22, 2011

Hitler: A Film from Germany, directed by Hans-Jürgen Syberberg (West Germany, France, UK, 1978)

An experimental film about the rise and fall of Nazism in Germany.

The Taking of Power by Louis XIV, directed by Roberto Rossellini (France, 1966)

A film about the rise to power of King Louis XIV of France.

Gomorra, directed by Matteo Garrone (Italy, 2008)

A drama focusing on the micro politics of a family-based organized crime syndicate in Naples, Italy.

I, Pierre Rivière, directed by René Allio (France, 1976)

A film based closely on a collection of historical documents edited by Foucault concerning the murder by a young peasant of his family and his memoir of his crime.

Back to Normandy, directed by Nicolas Philibert (France, 2007)

Nicolas Philibert, who worked on Allio's 1976 film, returns to Normandy thirty years later to find the local actors who performed in the film.

FILM PROGRAM, APRIL 10–25, 2011

Le Cercle de Minuit—Spécial Foucault (France, 1994)

Le Cercle de Minuit was a French television program that ran four nights a week from 1992 to 1999. This special episode is a tribute to Foucault and the impact of his life and work on those interviewed.

Le pain noir, directed by Serge Moati (France, 1974–1975)

An eight-episode miniseries broadcast on French television. A view of historical events from 1880 to 1936 as lived by Cathie, a fictional peasant from Limousin forced to become a worker in Limoges.

The Autobiography of Nicolae Ceaușescu, directed by Andrei Ujică (Romania, 2010)

A three-hour documentary covering twenty-five years in the life of Nicolae Ceaușescu, put together from over a thousand hours of archival footage.

Punishment Park, directed by Peter Watkins (USA, 1971)

A dystopian mockumentary drama with a European film crew documenting a "game" involving soldiers and law enforcement officers pursuing members of countercultural groups across a desert to reach an American flag.

Lacombe, Lucien, directed by Louis Malle (France, 1974)

The story of a teenage boy and his interactions with the Resistance and the Gestapo during the Occupation in France in 1944.

Lancelot of the Lake, directed by Robert Bresson (France, Italy, 1974)

A film in which Bresson applies his trademark minimalism to the Arthurian legend.

Avenge But One of My Two Eyes, directed by Avi Mograbi (Israel, 2005)

A documentary about the treatment of Palestinians by the Israeli Army and the complexities of the conflict.

The Death of Maria Malibran, directed by Werner Schroeter (West Germany, 1972)

An experimental film about the life and death of the famous nineteenth-century opera singer Maria Malibran, who died on stage.

Love Meetings, directed by Pier Paolo Pasolini (Italy, 1964)

A film in which Pasolini wanders the streets with a microphone and interviews passing people about their customs and institutions related to sex and love in Italy.

NOTES

TRANSLATOR'S PREFACE

1. Michel Foucault, *Dits et écrits*, 4 vols., ed. Daniel Defert, François Ewald, and Jacques Lagrange (Paris: Gallimard, 1994).

INTRODUCTION

1. This event took place between October 22 and 31, 2004, as part of the annual Autumn Festival in Paris and marked the twentieth anniversary of the death of the philosopher. The program, which includes a brief introduction by Serge Toubiana, can be found at http://lgm .meichler.free.fr/Nouveau%20dossier/foucault.pdf.
2. Michel Foucault, ed., *I, Pierre Rivière, Having Slaughtered My Mother, My Sister, and My Brother . . . : A Case of Parricide in the 19th Century*, trans. Frank Jellinek (Lincoln: University of Nebraska Press, 1982).
3. Michel Foucault, "Film, History, and Popular Memory," chapter 3 in this volume.
4. Michel Foucault, "Marguerite Duras: Memory Without Remembering"; "The Nondisciplinary Camera Versus Sade"; and "Werner Schroeter and Michel Foucault in Conversation," chaps. 4, 6, and 12, respectively, in this volume.
5. Michel Foucault, "The Return of Pierre Rivière," chapter 9 in this volume.
6. This book was originally accompanied by a program of films shown at the Villa Arson in Nice from February to June 2011. Organized in partnership with L'ECLAT (Lieu d'Expériences pour le Cinéma, les

Lettres, Arts et Technologies), the film division of PACA (Pôle Régional d'Education Artistique et de Formation au Cinéma), the program of films, including some that were very contemporary, used cinema to address problems that preoccupied Foucault in his own time. The program is included in the appendix.

1. WHAT FILM IS ABLE TO DO

1. Olivier Assayas, Alain Bergala, Pascal Bonitzer, Serge Daney, Daniele Dubroux, Jean-Jacques Henry, Serge Le Péron, Jean Narboni, Guy-Parick Sainderichin, Louis Skorecki, Charles Tesson, and Serge Toubiana, "Dictionnaire sans foi ni loi," *Cahiers du cinéma*, no. 325 (June 1981): 116. *Translator's note*: The entry is worth citing in full here. "Foucault, Michel. Philosopher. In 1974, the *Cahiers* interviewed him on the fashion for retro. In 1975 Foucault left the 14 Juillet-Bastille cinema, furious after seeing *Here and Elsewhere* (Godard 1976). The author of *Discipline and Punish* had no desire to be either disciplined or punished by Godard. His tastes in film were less twisted. Nonetheless, for us, he continues to be a constant, irreplaceable, and essential reference. At one time his personal work and the issues of the day led him to grant René Allio and him alone the film rights to the collection, *I Pierre Rivière . . . .*"

2. When asked about Hans-Jürgen Syberberg's film *Hitler: A Film from Germany* (1977), Foucault confirmed during an interview: "I'm not talking about the aesthetics of film here, which is something I know nothing about." Foucault was actually familiar with all of Syberberg's films, as the editors of *Dits et écrits* say in the preamble to the interview "The Four Horsemen of the Apocalypse" (chapter 11 in this volume). For this comment, see Michel Foucault, "Les quatre cavaliers de l'Apocalypse et les vermisseaux quotidiens," in *Dits et écrits*, ed. Daniel Defert, François Ewald, and Jacques Lagrange (Paris: Gallimard, 1994), 4:102.

3. Michel Foucault, *The Order of Things: An Archaeology of the Human Sciences*, trans. Alan Sheridan (London: Routledge Classics, 2002).

4. Michel Foucault, *Death and the Labyrinth: The World of Raymond Roussel*, trans. Charles Ruas (London: Athlone, 1987).

5. On these historical points, see Antoine de Baecque, *Les Cahiers du cinéma, histoire d'une revue*, vol. 2: *Cinéma, tours et détours, 1959–1981* (Paris: Cahiers du cinéma, Diffusion, Seuil, 1991), 78, 211, 219.

6. Michel Foucault, "Film, History and Popular Memory," chapter 3 in this volume.

7. Although Serge Daney's name is not included in the introduction to this interview as it was originally published in the *Cahiers* or mentioned in its republication in *Dits et écrits*, he was nonetheless present at the interview with Foucault. Michel Foucault, "Anti-Rétro. Entretien avec Michel Foucault," *Cahiers du cinéma*, no. 251–52 (July–August 1974): 5–15. Republished as Michel Foucault, "Anti-Rétro," in Michel Foucault, *Dits et écrits*, 2:646–60. For a further elaboration by Serge Daney on the notion of "the fashion for retro," see "Anti-Rétro (suite) et fonction critique (fin)," *Cahiers du cinéma*, no. 253 (October–November 1974): 20–36. Also published in Serge Daney, *La Maison cinéma et le monde, 1. Le temps des* Cahiers *1962–1981*, ed. Patrice Rollet (Paris: POL, coll. Trafic, 2001).

8. Serge Toubiana, "Michel Foucault et le cinéma," in *Michel Foucault, la littérature et les arts*, ed. Philippe Artières (Paris: Kimé, 2004), 192.

9. Michel Foucault, "Foreword," in *I, Pierre Rivière, Having Slaughtered My Mother, My Sister, and My Brother . . . : A Case of Parricide in the 19th Century*, ed. Michel Foucault, trans. Frank Jellinek (Lincoln: University of Nebraska Press, 1982), vii–viii.

10. Foucault, "Foreword," xii. Foucault declared that Rivière's case "literally reduced criminologists, psychologists, and psychiatrists . . . to silence." "Crime and Discourse," chapter 8 in this volume.

11. Daney, "Anti-Rétro," 36.

12. Daney, "Anti-Rétro," 36.

13. Foucault, "Film, History, and Popular Memory."

14. Foucault, "Film, History, and Popular Memory."

15. Daney, "Anti-Rétro," 36.

16. Daney, "Anti-Rétro," 36.

17. Michel Foucault, "The Nondisciplinary Camera Versus Sade," chapter 6 in this volume.

18. Foucault, "The Four Horsemen of the Apocalypse."

19. Foucault, "Film, History, and Popular Memory."

20. Michel Foucault, "The Return of Pierre Rivière," chapter 9 in this volume.

21. Michel Foucault, *The History of Sexuality*, vol. 1: *An Introduction*, trans. Robert Hurley (New York: Pantheon, 1978), 90. *Translator's note:* This book has multiple titles in English. The 1998 Penguin edition is titled *The Will to Know. The History of Sexuality: 1.*

22. Michel Foucault, "The Dull Regime of Tolerance," chapter 10 in this volume.

23. Michel Foucault, "Werner Schroeter and Michel Foucault in Conversation," chapter 12 in this volume.

24. Foucault, "The Nondisciplinary Camera."

25. Michel Foucault, *The History of Sexuality*, vol. 2: *The Use of Pleasure*, trans. Robert Hurley (London: Penguin, 1985); Michel Foucault, *The History of Sexuality*, vol. 3: *The Care of the Self*, trans. Robert Hurley (London: Penguin, 1990).

26. Foucault, "Werner Schroeter."

27. Michel Foucault, "The Asylum and the Carnival," chapter 7 in this volume.

28. Michel Foucault, *Discipline and Punish*, trans. Alan Sheridan (London: Penguin, 1991). Originally published in French in 1975.

29. Foucault, "The Asylum and the Carnival."

30. Foucault, "The Return of Pierre Rivière."

31. *Translator's note*: René Allio's film will be referred to henceforth by the title of the DVD released in Britain in 2008 by Tartan Films.

32. Foucault, *The Order of Things*, chapter 1.

33. Michel Foucault, *This Is Not a Pipe: With Illustrations and Letters by René Magritte*, ed. and trans. James Harkness (Berkeley: University of California Press, 1983).

34. *Translator's note*: A version of this work on Manet is published in Michel Foucault, *Manet and the Object of Painting*, trans. Matthew Barr (London: Tate, 2011). Foucault signed a contract in 1967 to publish a book on Manet with Éditions de Minuit but never delivered. In a review of the 2011 book above, Suzanne Verderber (*Foucault Studies* 19 [2015]: 266) draws attention to the history and different reports around this proposed monograph. She says that Maryvonne Saison, editor of the French edition (Michel Foucault, *La Peinture de Manet*

[Paris: Éditions de Minuit, 2004]), "claims the projected Manet book was to be entitled *Le noir et la couleur*, and Bourriaud [in the English edition] claims it is *Le noir et la surface*, as does Didier Éribon, in *Michel Foucault*, trans. Betsy Wing (Cambridge, Mass.: Harvard University Press, 1991), 190."

35. Foucault, "The Return of Pierre Rivière."
36. Foucault, "The Asylum and the Carnival."
37. Michel Foucault, "Marguerite Duras: Memory Without Remembering," chapter 4 in this volume.
38. Marguerite Duras, *Moderato cantabile*, trans. Richard Seaver (Richmond: Oneworld Classics, 2008).
39. Foucault, "Marguerite Duras."
40. Michel Foucault, *History of Madness*, ed. Jean Khalfa, trans. Jonathan Murphy and Jean Khalfa (London: Routledge, 2006).
41. Mathieu Potte-Bonneville has drawn attention very well to the role of some of the literary references in this first book of Foucault's. These references, he says, "testify to the constant presence of an experience and a rupture from within which institutions and theories can be interpreted beyond the forms of institutional care or theoretical debate." Potte-Bonneville, *Michel Foucault, l'inquietude de l'histoire* (Paris: PUF, 2004), 76.
42. Foucault, "The Nondisciplinary Camera."
43. Foucault, *The History of Sexuality*, 1:157, 159.
44. On the "grip of power," see Foucault, *The History of Sexuality*, 1:157.
45. Foucault, "The Nondisciplinary Camera."
46. Foucault, "The Dull Regime of Tolerance."
47. Foucault, *The History of Sexuality*, 1:157.
48. Foucault, "Werner Schroeter."
49. In "The Nondisciplinary Camera," concerning the representation of the body in Schroeter, Foucault has this to say: "It is an 'unnameable' and 'unusable' thing, existing beyond all programs of desire; *it is a body rendered entirely plastic by pleasure*: something that opens, stretches, throbs, beats, and gapes. When we see two women embrace in *The Death of Maria Malibran*, we see dunes, a desert caravan, a voracious advancing flower, insect mandibles, a grassy crevice" (emphasis added).
50. Foucault, "The Nondisciplinary Camera."

51. See Clement Greenberg, *Art and Culture: Critical Essays* (Boston: Beacon, 1961).

52. Foucault, "Marguerite Duras."

53. Foucault, "The Nondisciplinary Camera."

54. Foucault, "The Nondisciplinary Camera."

55. Foucault, "The Nondisciplinary Camera."

56. Foucault, "Marguerite Duras."

57. Foucault, "The Asylum and the Carnival."

58. Foucault, "Crime and Discourse."

59. Serge Daney, "'Uranus' le deuil du deuil," in Daney, *Devant la recrudescence des vols de sacs à main. Cinéma, télévision, information: 1988–1991* (Lyon: Aléas, 1991), 154.

60. Foucault, "The Return of Pierre Rivière."

61. In a passage where he compares Bergman and Schroeter, Foucault says: "When I see a film by Bergman, who is also a filmmaker obsessed with women and by love between women, I'm bored. Bergman bores me, because I think he wants to try and see what is going on between these women. Whereas with you, there's a kind of immediacy that doesn't try to show what's happening, and which means the question is not even raised. And your way of completely avoiding the psychological film seems fruitful to me. Instead, we see bodies, faces, lips and eyes." Foucault, "Werner Schroeter."

62. See, for example, André Bazin, "William Wyler, or the Jansenist of Directing," in *Bazin at Work: Major Essays and Reviews from the Forties and Fifties*, ed. Bert Cardullo, trans. Alain Piette and Bert Cardullo (London: Routledge, 1997), 1–22.

63. See Gilles Deleuze, *Cinema 1: The Movement-Image*, trans. Hugh Tomlinson and Barbara Habberjam (Minneapolis: University of Minnesota Press, 1986).

64. Michel Foucault, *The Archaeology of Knowledge and the Discourse on Language*, trans. A. M. Sheridan Smith (New York: Pantheon, 1972), 130.

65. Foucault, *The Archaeology of Knowledge*, 130–31.

66. Potte-Bonneville, *Michel Foucault*, 76.

67. Foucault. "The Four Horsemen of the Apocalypse."

68. Gilles Deleuze, "What Is a Dispositif?" in *Michel Foucault Philosopher*, ed. T. J. Armstrong (Hemel Hempstead: Harvester Wheatsheaf, 1992), 165–66 (emphasis added).

69. Foucault, "The Return of Pierre Rivière."

70. Foucault, "Film, History, and Popular Memory" (Foucault's emphasis).

71. Foucault, "Film, History, and Popular Memory."

72. Foucault, *The Archaeology of Knowledge*, 9.

73. Foucault, *The Archaeology of Knowledge*, 10.

74. On the series and the event in Foucault, see chapter 2.

75. On all these points, see Foucault, *The Archaeology of Knowledge*, 9–10.

76. Michel Foucault, "The Order of Discourse," in *Untying the Text: A Poststructuralist Reader*, ed. R. Young, trans. Ian McLeod (Boston: Routledge and Kegan Paul, 1981), 68.

77. Foucault, "The Four Horsemen of the Apocalypse" (Foucault's emphasis).

78. For a brief definition by Foucault of his notion of "problematization," see "The Concern for Truth," in *Foucault Live: Collected Interviews, 1961–1984*, ed. Sylvère Lotringer, trans. John Johnston (New York: Semiotext(e), 1996), 456–57.

79. Foucault, "The Return of Pierre Rivière."

80. Foucault, "The Four Horsemen of the Apocalypse."

81. Daney, "'Uranus' le deuil du deuil," 154. For Daney, this was a way of continuing a reflection that began with the criticism of the fashion for retro, directly inspired by Foucault, and which continued in the previously cited article, "Anti-Retro," 35–36. Bearing in mind the development of a "memory of popular struggles," Daney stigmatizes all "forgetting" and all "liquidation" of the past in films that take the path of "removing guilt" or of creating a "clear conscience" (such as *The Night Porter*).

82. Foucault, "The Four Horsemen of the Apocalypse."

83. Foucault, "Film, History, and Popular Memory" (Foucault's emphasis).

84. Michel Foucault, "Preface," in Gilles Deleuze and Félix Guattari, *Anti-Oedipus, Capitalism and Schizophrenia*, trans. Robert Hurley, Mark Seem, and Helen R. Lane (Minneapolis: University of Minnesota Press, 1983), xiii–xiv.

85. *Translator's note*: This is a reference to the title of Foucault's collected shorter works in French, *Dits et écrits*.

86. Gilles Deleuze, *Foucault*, trans. and ed. Séan Hand (London: Continuum, 1999), 70.

206 ∥ 1. WHAT FILM IS ABLE TO DO

87. *Translator's note*: A. M. Sheridan Smith, translator of *The Archaeology of Knowledge*, translates the French word *rémanence* as "remanence" and *rémanent* as "residual," with the original French words in brackets. Given the film context here, I am rendering this word as "persistence" as a reference to the notion of the "persistence of vision," an old and now superseded scientific theory concerning the retention of an image after the initial stimulus, used to account for the illusion of movement in film. The word is also used in computing in French to designate "nonvolatile" memory, secondary long-term persistent storage that persists even after the computer has been shut down. It is very much in this sense that Foucault is using the word in *The Archaeology of Knowledge*. "To say that statements are residual (*rémanent*) is not to say that they remain in the field of memory, or that it is possible to rediscover what they meant; but it means that they are preserved by virtue of a number of supports and material techniques (of which the book is, of course, only one example), in accordance with certain types of institutions." Foucault, *The Archaeology of Knowledge*, 123.
88. Foucault, "The Order of Discourse," 68.
89. Foucault, "The Return of Pierre Rivière." The use of *Blow-Up* (1967) could also serve as a way of distinguishing between Foucault's practice of history and that of the Annales school. See in this regard the interview with Jacques Revel (which does not deal with Foucault) titled "Un exercise de désorientement: *Blow Up*," in *De l'histoire au cinéma*, ed. Antoine de Baecque and Christian Delage (Paris: Complex, 2008), 99–110.
90. Foucault, "The Asylum and the Carnival."
91. Gilles Deleuze, "Foucault and Prisons," in *Two Regimes of Madness: Texts and Interviews 1975–1995*, ed. David Lapoujade, trans. Ames Hodges and Mike Taormina (New York: Semiotext(e)/Foreign Agents, 2007), 274.

2. VERSIONS OF THE PRESENT

1. That doesn't mean he didn't comment on the *specificity* of film, as chapter 1 demonstrates. But this specificity is linked not to the correct conceptual qualification of an object to be described in itself but to the particular challenge that film can represent for a philosophical

process engaged in a particular program, in this case the Foucauldian enterprise itself.

2. *Translator's note*: "I've always been interested in technique, not in art for technique's sake. In the last installments of 'Histoire(s) du cinéma,' I keep saying—or often have it said—that cinema is neither an art nor a technique, but a mystery." Jean-Luc Godard, press conference at the Montreal Film Festival in 1995, transcribed by Henri Béhar, *Film Scouts*, http://www.filmscouts.com/scripts/interview.cfm?ArticleCode=2800.

3. Michel Foucault, "Werner Schroeter and Michel Foucault in Conversation," chapter 12 in this volume.

4. This idea of the encounter is inspired by Gilles Deleuze. See, for example, the lecture "What Is the Creative Act?" in *Two Regimes of Madness: Texts and Interviews 1975–1995*, ed. David Lapoujade, trans. Ames Hodges and Mike Taormina (New York: Semiotext(e)/Foreign Agents, 2007), 321–24. For an exposition of this idea, which runs right through Deleuze's work from *Difference and Repetition* until his final texts, and more generally in relation to the encounter between film and philosophy in Deleuze, see Dork Zabunyan, *Gilles Deleuze: Voir, parler, penser au risque du cinéma* (Paris: Presse Nouvelle Sorbonne, 2008).

5. Paul Veyne, "Foucault Revolutionizes History," in *Foucault and His Interlocutors*, ed. Arnold I. Davidson (Chicago: University of Chicago Press, 1997). For a stimulating rereading of this revolution through its effects on literary history, see Marie Gil, "Foucault invente l'histoire litteraire," *Fabula LHT (litterature, histoire, theorie)*, no. 0 (2005), http://www.fabula.org/lht/0/Gil.html.

6. "Genealogy does not pretend to go back in time to restore an unbroken continuity that operates beyond the dispersion of forgotten things; its duty is not to demonstrate that the past actively exists in the present, that it continues secretly to animate the present, having imposed a predetermined form on all its vicissitudes." Michel Foucault, "Nietzsche, Genealogy, History," in *The Foucault Reader*, ed. Paul Rabinow (New York: Pantheon, 1984), 81.

7. Foucault, "Nietzsche, Genealogy, History," 89.

8. Foucault, "Nietzsche, Genealogy, History," 93.

9. "History becomes 'effective' to the degree that it introduces discontinuity into our very being." Foucault, "Nietzsche, Genealogy, History," 88.

10. Foucault, "Nietzsche, Genealogy, History," 87.
11. *Translator's note*: The Groupe d'Information sur les Prisons (GIP) was an activist group founded in 1970 by Michel Foucault, Jean-Marie Domenach, and Pierre Vidal-Naquet with the aim of gathering and distributing information about conditions in French prisons and giving prisoners a voice. For a collection of documents produced by this group, see Collectif, *Intolérable. Textes réunis par le Groupe d'Information sur les Prisons*, ed. Philippe Artières (Paris: Collection Verticales, Gallimard, 2013).
12. *Translator's note*: "I believe that the job of a cop is to exert physical force. Whoever opposes the cops shouldn't allow them to get away with the hypocrisy of hiding under orders which we need to obey immediately. They need to follow through on what they represent." Michel Foucault, "Aller à Madrid," in *Dits et écrits*, ed. Daniel Defert, François Ewald, and Jacques Lagrange (Paris: Gallimard, 1994), 2:761.
13. On these concepts, see in particular Michel Foucault, *The Archaeology of Knowledge and the Discourse on Language*, trans. A. M. Sheridan Smith (New York: Pantheon, 1972), 68–60, 175, 185, 194.
14. I have elaborated at length on this method in relation to metaphysics in Patrice Maniglier, "Manifeste pour un comparatisme supérieur en philosophie," *Temps Modernes*, no. 682 (July 2015): 86–145.
15. Michel Foucault, "Film, History, and Popular Memory," chapter 3 in this volume.
16. Foucault, "Film, History, and Popular Memory."
17. Serge Daney, "Anti-Rétro (suite) et fonction critique (fin)," *Cahiers du cinéma*, no. 253 (October–November 1974): 36.
18. The importance of this theme of a history written from the point of view of those who are involved in it, for the encounter between cinema and philosophy around May 1968, is particularly well highlighted by Dork Zabunyan in a text to which the current chapter owes much: "Un effet de blow up: philosophie, cinema et inconscient de l'histoire," in *Le Moment philosophique des années soixante*, ed. Patrice Maniglier (Paris: PUF, 2011).
19. Foucault, "Film, History, and Popular Memory."
20. Foucault, "Film, History, and Popular Memory."
21. Louis Althusser, *Reply to John Lewis*, trans. Grahame Locke (London: NLB, 1976), 57; and Louis Althusser, *For Marx*, trans. Ben Brewster (London: Allen Lane, Penguin, 1969), section on "Marxism

and Humanism," 219ff. See also Étienne Balibar's wonderful contribution dedicated to Marx's theory of history in *Reading Capital*. It is a text that in many ways anticipates the problems raised by Foucault and Deleuze, showing as it does that history is not the history *of* something (even of humanity) but the constantly renewed relaunching of a different combination of "factors": Balibar, "The Basic Concepts of Historical Materialism," in *Reading Capital: The Complete Edition*, by Louis Althusser, Etienne Balibar, Roger Establet, Pierre Macherey, and Jacques Rancière, trans. Ben Brewster and David Fernbach (London: Verso, 2016).

22. See what Sartre has to say in *Words* about the "retrospective illusion" that reigns over the history of great men, and in particular this striking passage: "In the drawing-rooms of Arras, a cold and affected young lawyer is carrying his head under his arm because he is the late Robespierre; the head is dripping blood, though it does not stain the carpet; not one of the guests notices it, yet we see nothing else; some five years go by before it rolled into the basket, and yet there it is, chopped off, making gallant speeches, in spite of its sagging jaw." Jean-Paul Sartre, *Words*, trans. Irene Clephane (London: Penguin Modern Classics 2000), 126. Actually, many historical films fall within the ambit of this illusion.

23. As we know, all this underlies the *Annales* approach of Fernand Braudel, Marc Bloch, Pierre Chaunu, and others who claimed to be historians of the anonymous.

24. *Translator's note*: On "subjugated knowledge," see Michel Foucault, *"Society Must Be Defended": Lectures at the Collège de France*, ed. Mauro Bertani and Alessandro Fontana, trans. David Macey (New York: Picador, 2001), 7–9.

25. "The perception that Western man has of his own time and space allows a structure of refusal to appear, on the basis of which a discourse is denounced as not being language, a gesture as not being an *oeuvre*, a figure as having no rightful place in history. . . . The *necessity of madness* throughout the history of the West is linked to that decisive action that extracts a significant language from the background noise and its continuous monotony, a language which is transmitted and culminates in time; it is in short, linked to the *possibility of history*. The structure of the experience of madness, which is a history through

and through, but whose seat is at its margins, where its decisions are made is the object of this study." Michel Foucault, *History of Madness*, ed. Jean Khalfa, trans. Jonathan Murphy and Jean Khalfa (London: Routledge, 2006), xxxii. Admittedly, Foucault removed this preface from later editions, but not because he had abandoned the project of a *critical* history; rather, because the formulations seemed to him to be still too closely related to phenomenological problematics that turned madness into a kind of timeless object. But it is precisely a question of thinking about a nonhistorical change and not an eternity in the face of which discourse would always fail.

26. Michel Foucault, "Lives of Infamous Men," in *Essential Works of Foucault, 1954–1984*, vol. 3: *Power*, ed. J. Faubion, trans. Robert Hurley (New York: New Press, 2000), 157–75. This article was originally published in French in 1977.

27. "Lives of Infamous Men," 166.

28. "Lives of Infamous Men," 157.

29. The entire passage that follows is a loose commentary on a famous article by Foucault, his true philosophical testament, "What Is Enlightenment?" in *Essential Works of Foucault, 1954–1984*, vol. 1: *Ethics: Subjectivity and Truth*, ed. Paul Rabinow, trans. Catherine Porter (New York: New Press, 1997), 303–19.

30. It's not alone: anthropology is also a critical discipline (I think this is how Lévi-Strauss should be read). Law can also function in this way (as Marcela Iacub's books have shown recently). A critical sociology is certainly possible (Latour's rather than Bourdieu's), and, as we will attempt to show in the following pages, film can also function as critique. In short, critique is a general form of knowledge and is not limited to such and such a discipline in particular, even if it's true that not all knowledge is capable of taking a critical turn.

31. On this interpretation of anthropology and its Lévi-Straussian antecedents, see my article "Anthropological Meditations: The Discourse on Comparative Method," in *Anthropology After Metaphysics*, ed. Pierre Charbonnier, Gildas Salmon, and Peter Skafish (Lanham, Md.: Rowman & Littlefield, 2016), 109–32. See also Eduardo Viveiros de Castro, *Cannibal Metaphysics*, ed. and trans. Peter Skafish (Minneapolis: Univocal, 2014).

32. Michel Foucault, *The History of Sexuality*, vol. 2: *The Use of Pleasure*, trans. Robert Hurley (Harmondsworth: Penguin, 1992), 8.

33. Claude Lévi-Strauss, *Structural Anthropology*, trans. Monique Layton (New York: Basic Books, 1976), 2:272.

34. Marc Bloch, *The Historian's Craft*, trans. Peter Putnam (Manchester: Manchester University Press, 1992), 23.

35. Foucault, "Nietzsche, Genealogy, History," 379.

36. Foucault, "Nietzsche, Genealogy, History," 380.

37. Gilles Deleuze, *Difference and Repetition*, trans. Paul Patton (New York: Columbia University Press, 1994), 156.

38. Michel Foucault, "The Order of Discourse," in *Untying the Text: A Poststructuralist Reader*, ed. R. Young, trans. Ian McLeod (Boston: Routledge and Kegan Paul, 1981), 69.

39. Gilles Deleuze, *The Logic of Sense*, ed. Constantin V. Boundas, trans. Mark Lester with Charles Stivale (New York: Columbia University Press, 1993).

40. Foucault, "The Order of Discourse," 69.

41. Foucault writes that the first act of archaeology is "to restore to the statement the specificity of its occurrence," as it "emerges in its historical irruption; what we try to examine is the incision that it makes, that irreducible—and very often tiny—emergence." Foucault, *The Archaeology of Knowledge*, 28.

42. "The fundamental notions which we now require . . . are those of the event and the series, along with the notions which are linked to them: regularity, dimension of chance (aléa), discontinuity, dependence, transformation." Foucault, "The Order of Discourse," 68.

43. Foucault, *The Archaeology of Knowledge*, 40.

44. Michel Foucault, *Discipline and Punish: The Birth of the Prison*, trans. Alan Sheridan (New York: Vintage, 1995).

45. See Foucault, *History of Madness*; and Michel Foucault, *Psychiatric Power: Lectures at the Collège de France 1973–1974*, ed. Jacques Lagrange, trans. Graham Burchell (Basingstoke: Palgrave Macmillan, 2006).

46. Foucault, *The Archaeology of Knowledge*, 41.

47. "Whereas in previous periods madness was carefully distinguished from criminal conduct and was regarded as an excuse, criminality itself becomes—and subsequent to the celebrated 'homicidal

monomanias'—a form of deviance more or less related to madness."
Foucault, *The Archaeology of Knowledge*, 41.

48. Michel Foucault, *The Order of Things: An Archaeology of the Human Sciences*, trans. Alan Sheridan (London: Routledge Classics, 2002), 420–22. I provided a thorough reading of *The Order of Things* along the line of this (admittedly structuralist) interpretation in "Foucault and The Order of Things," in *A Companion to Michel Foucault*, ed. Christopher Falzon, Timothy O'Leary, and Jana Sawicki (London: Wiley-Blackwell, 2013), 104–35.

49. It is interesting to note that this image of film, which, as we know, allowed Henri Bergson to characterize a certain conception of change as a succession of states, is also the image Marc Bloch uses to characterize the time that the historian must go back through. Marc Bloch, *French Rural History: An Essay on Its Basic Characteristics*, trans. Janet Sondheimer (London: Routledge, 2015), xxx.

50. Foucault defines "eventalization" in "Questions of Method," in *Essential Works of Foucault, 1954–1984*, vol. 3: *Power*, ed. James D. Faubion (New York: New Press, 2000), 226–29.

51. See Michel Foucault, *The History of Sexuality*, vol. 1: *An Introduction*, trans. Robert Hurley (New York: Pantheon, 1978), 94–96; and Michel Foucault, "Power, Moral Values and the Intellectual," *History of the Present* 4 (1988): 1–2, 11–13.

52. Gilles Deleuze, *Foucault*, ed. and trans. Seán Hand (London: Athlone, 1988), 34.

53. See in particular the article by Sergei Eisenstein, "A Dialectic Approach to Film Form," in *Film Form: Essays in Film Theory*, ed. and trans. Jay Leda (New York: Harcourt, 1977), 45–63.

54. Dziga Vertov, "Kinoks, a Revolution," in *Kino-Eye: The Writings of Dziga Vertov*, ed. and intro. Annette Michelson, trans. Kevin O'Brien (Berkeley: University of California Press, 1984), 16.

55. Vertov, "Kinoks, a Revolution," 18.

56. Vertov, "Kino-Eye," in *Kino-Eye*, 69.

57. Vertov, "Kinoks, a Revolution," 16.

58. Vertov, "From Kino-Eye to Radio-Eye," in *Kino-Eye*, 90–91.

59. Gilles Deleuze, *Cinema 1: The Movement-Image*, trans. Hugh Tomlinson and Barbara Habberjam (Minneapolis: University of Minnesota

Press, 1986); and Gilles Deleuze, *Cinema 2: The Time Image*, trans. Hugh Tomlinson and Robert Galeta (Minneapolis: University of Minneapolis Press, 1989).

60. Foucault, "Film, History, and Popular Memory."

61. Serge Toubiana confirmed in an interview that he was kind enough to grant us that it was he who gave a copy of Foucault's book to Allio. There is a trace in Allio's *Carnets* published after his death of Allio's immediate and enthusiastic reading: "12/2/74: Reading *I, Pierre Rivière, Having Slaughtered* etc. . . . by Foucault's team. It's a story of this kind, with this kind of violence, talking about what it talks about, that needs to be spoken about: see the faits divers." René Allio, *Carnets* (Paris: Lieu Commun, 1991), 39.

62. Allio, *Carnets*, 42.

63. On the generality of the Foucauldian process as Allio perceived it, see the long reflection on what he himself calls "the Foucault effect" in art, where he compares this process to Brechtian distantiation. Allio, *Carnets*, 46–48.

64. Foucault, "The Return of Pierre Rivière," chapter 9 in this volume.

65. This text has seen two publications in French: the first in 1968, republished in the first volume of *Dits et écrits*; the second version, a reworked edition published in 1973 by Fata Morgana. The latter is used here: *Translator's note*: The English translation is of this latter text.

66. Michel Foucault, *This Is Not a Pipe: With Illustrations and Letters by René Magritte*, ed. and trans. James Harkness (Berkeley: University of California Press, 1983), 26. I am relying on the very fine commentary by Lucien Vinciguerra, "Comment inverser exactement Les Ménines: Michel Foucault et la peinture à la fin des années 1960, des formes symboliques aux dispositifs," in *Le moment philosophique des années 1960 en France*, ed. Patrice Maniglier (Paris: PUF, 2011), 477–94, which I refer to for a more complete reading of this text.

67. See Michel Foucault, *The Birth of the Clinic*, trans. A. M. Sheridan (London: Tavistock, 1973); and Foucault, *Discipline and Punish*, chapter 3, "Panopticism."

68. Deleuze, *Foucault*, 64–65.

69. Deleuze, *Cinema 2*.

70. On this, see Deleuze, *Cinema 2*, 247, and the explicit reference to Foucault on p. 246. A precise study of these texts can be found in the last part of Zabunyan's previously mentioned book, *Gilles Deleuze*.

71. "And in fact Allio does not simply use a voice-off but employs several different means in order to give a perceptible effect to the discrepancies or even dysfunctions between what is seen and what is articulated, the visual image (from the first shot, we see a tree in the deserted countryside, while we hear the noises and speeches of a common court)." Deleuze, *Foucault*, 141, n. 26.

72. It is important to note that none of this is arbitrarily introduced by Allio: all these phrases are in the testimony of witnesses.

73. Foucault, "The Return of Pierre Rivière."

74. Foucault, "The Return of Pierre Rivière."

75. Foucault, "Crime and Discourse," chapter 8 in this volume.

76. Marcel Mauss, "The Techniques of the Body," trans. Ben Brewster, *Economy and Society* 2, no. 1 (1973): 72.

77. Foucault, "Marguerite Duras: Memory Without Remembering," chapter 4 in this volume.

78. Deleuze, *Difference and Repetition*, 156.

79. Foucault, "Marguerite Duras."

80. Michel Foucault, "On the Ways of Writing History," in *Essential Works of Foucault, 1954–1984*, vol. 2: *Aesthetics, Method and Epistemology*, ed. James Faubion, trans. Robert Hurley (New York: New Press, 1998), 291. Translation modified.

81. Foucault, *Discipline and Punish*, 308.

82. Foucault, "The Nondisciplinary Camera Versus Sade," chapter 6 in this volume.

83. Foucault, "Werner Schroeter."

84. Foucault, "The Nondisciplinary Camera."

85. One could also cite Balázs, for whom film "showed us the face of things, the play of nature's features, the microdrama of physiognomies and mass gestures." Béla Balázs, *Béla Balázs: Early Film Theory. Visible Man and the Spirit of Film*, ed. Erica Carter, trans. Rodney Livingstone (New York: Berghahn, 2010), 184. *Translator's note*: For a useful article on the use of the term *photogénie* by the French impressionistic cinema movement and by Jean Epstein in particular, see

Robert Farmer, "Jean Epstein," *Senses of Cinema* 57 (December 2010), http://sensesofcinema.com/2010/great-directors/jean-epstein/.

86. Jean Epstein, "Cinema and Modern Literature," in *Jean Epstein: Critical Essays and New Translations*, ed. Sarah Keller and Jason N. Paul (Amsterdam: Amsterdam University Press, 2012), 272–73.

87. Jean Epstein, *Écrits sur le cinéma, 1921–1953: édition chronologique en deux volumes*, vol. 1: *1921–1947*, ed. Pierre Lherminier (Paris: Cinéma Club/Seghers, 1975), 87.

88. Epstein, "Cinema and Modern Literature," 273.

89. Epstein, *Écrits sur le cinéma*, 94.

90. Epstein, *Écrits sur le cinéma*, 87.

91. Epstein, "Cinema and Modern Literature," 274.

92. Epstein, *Écrits sur le cinéma*, 86. *Translator's note*: This passage appears in translation in Jacques Rancière, *Film Fables*, trans. Emiliano Battista (Oxford: Berg, 2006), 1.

93. Epstein, *Écrits sur le cinéma*, 91.

94. See the prologue to Rancière, *Film Fables*, 1ff.

95. See André Bazin, "Will CinemaScope Save the Film Industry? (1953)," *Film-Philosophy* 6, no. 2 (January 2002), http://www.film-philosophy.com/index.php/f-p/article/view/666/579.

96. This interview was published for the first time in Richard Raskin, *Nuit et Brouillard: On the Making, Reception and Functions of a Major Documentary Film* (Aarhus: Aarhus University Press, 1987). The interview appears in French in this book. The interview and other material from the book can also be found in the sixty-page booklet that accompanies the DVD release by Arte Video in 2003. For a history of the film, see Sylvie Lindeperg, *"Night and Fog": A Film in History*, trans. Tom Mes (Minnesota: University of Minnesota Press, 2014). For a good analysis, see Antoine de Baecque, *L'histoire-camera* (Paris: Gallimard, 2008).

97. Alain Resnais, "Interview with Alain Resnais," in Raskin, *Nuit et Brouillard*, 51.

98. On this meaning of the word "conversion," which I have borrowed from Étienne Balibar's reading of Hegel, see Balibar, *Violence and Civility: On the Limits of Political Philosophy*, trans. G. M. Goshgarian (New York: Columbia University Press, 2016).

99. Resnais, "Interview with Alain Resnais," 63, 59–60.

100. As Resnais says: "And most important, in France we were in the middle of the Algerian war and the Algerian war was spreading to France. There were already zones in the middle of France where there were internment camps—okay they weren't concentration camps—but already drivers weren't being allowed to stop their cars as they drove past," and so on. Resnais, "Interview with Alain Resnais," 51. Cayrol also remarks, "Don't forget that our own country is not free of racist scandal." Jean Cayrol, "Nous avons conçu 'Nuit et brouillard' comme un dispositive d'alerte," in Raskin, *Nuit et Brouillard*, 137.

101. See again Resnais's testimony, "Interview with Alain Resnais," 57.

102. Resnais, "Interview with Alain Resnais," 61.

103. See Hannah Arendt, *Eichmann in Jerusalem: A Report on the Banality of Evil* (New York: Viking, 1964).

104. *Translator's note*: For a definition by Foucault of his notion of "problematization," see "The Concern for Truth," in *Foucault Live: Collected Interviews, 1961–1984*, ed. Sylvère Lotringer, trans. John Johnston (New York: Semiotext(e), 1996), 455–64.

105. Richard Raskin, "Shooting Script," in Raskin, *Nuit et Brouillard*, 130.

106. Raskin, "Shooting Script," 88.

107. The term "surface of emergence" is borrowed from Foucault, *The Archaeology of Knowledge*, 41.

108. Raskin, "Shooting Script," 96–97.

109. Foucault, "What Is Enlightenment?" 303–19.

110. *Translator's note*: Since writing the current chapter, Patrice Maniglier has coauthored extended analyses of both Tarantino's film and Claude Lanzmann's film *Shoah* (1985). See Marie Gil and Patrice Maniglier, "L'image-vengeance: Tarantino face à l'histoire. Inglourious Basterds," in *Quentin Tarantino: Un cinéma déchaîné*, ed. Emmanuel Burdeau and Nicolas Vieillescazes (Paris: Capricci/Les Prairies ordinaires, 2013), 100–121; and Patrice Maniglier, "Lanzmann philosophe (Introduction au corps-Shoah)," in *Claude Lanzmann: Un voyant dans le siècle*, ed. Juliette Simont (Paris: Gallimard, 2017).

111. "Vicious" is the term that Foucault uses to talk about Manet: Michel Foucault, *Manet and the Object of Painting*, trans. Matthew Barr (London: Tate, 2009; 2011), 55, and Lucien Vinciguerra also applies to

Magritte: Vinciguerra, "Comment inverser exactement Les Ménines."
Foucault for his part speaks of a kind of cold cruelty in Magritte. See
This Is Not a Pipe.

3. FILM, HISTORY, AND POPULAR MEMORY

This interview conducted by the editors of *Cahiers du cinéma*, Pascal
Bonitzer, Serge Toubiana, and Serge Daney, was published in 1974:
Michel Foucault, "Anti-Rétro," entretien avec Michel Foucault, *Cahiers
du cinéma*, no. 251–52 (July–August 1974): 5–15. It was republished in
Michel Foucault, *Dits et écrits*, ed. Daniel Defert, François Ewald, and
Jacques Lagrange (Paris: Gallimard, 1994), 2:646–60. Although not
named in either of these publications, Daney also participated in this
interview.

1. *Translator's note*: In the short introduction that prefaces this interview in its original publication in the *Cahiers*, Bonitzer and Toubiana describe "retro" as a "snobbish fetishism for all that's old
   (clothes and décor) combined with a mockery of history." Foucault,
   "Anti-Retro," 5.

2. *Translator's note*: André Tardieu was a conservative prime minister of
   France for three terms between 1929 and 1932.

3. *Translator's note*: *Dossiers de l'écran* (Screen files) was a fortnightly,
   then monthly, program that ran on French television from 1967 to
   1991. Its format was the broadcast of a film, followed by a debate.

4. *Translator's note*: LIP was a watch factory in Besançon in France, which,
   after experiencing financial difficulties, decided to restructure and fire
   450 workers. It became a famous point of reference in France when,
   after strikes and the occupation of the factory in 1973, it came to be
   managed by the workers.

5. *Paths of Glory*, directed by Stanley Kubrick, USA, 1957. *Translator's
   note*: This film was banned in France until 1975, a year after this interview, because of its less than flattering portrait of the French Army
   during World War I.

6. *Translator's note*: This is a reference to Georges Bataille, "The Notion
   of Expenditure," in *Visions of Excess Selected Writings, 1927–1939*, ed.
   Allan Stoekl, trans. Allan Stoekl, Carl R. Lovitt, and Donald M.
   Leslie Jr. (Minneapolis: University of Minnesota Press, 1985).

7. Michel Foucault, ed., *I, Pierre Rivière, Having Slaughtered My Mother, My Sister, and My Brother . . . : A Case of Parricide in the 19th Century*, trans. Frank Jellinek (Lincoln: University of Nebraska Press, 1982).

8. *Translator's note*: Louis Malle and the novelist Patrick Modiano worked together on the screenplay for the film. Modiano won the Nobel Prize for Literature in 2014.

9. *The Night of San Juan*, directed by Jorge Sanjinés, Bolivia, 1971. A Bolivian and Italian coproduction on the struggles of Bolivian tin miners in 1967.

10. *Ein Leben Lang*, directed by Gustav Ucicky, Germany, 1940.

11. *The Sorrow and the Pity*, directed by Marcel Ophüls, France, 1969; *Français si vous saviez*, directed by André Harris and Alain de Sedouy, France, 1973.

12. *Translator's note*: Jacques Duclos (1896–1975) was a notable communist politician who played a key role in French politics from 1926 to 1969.

13. Louis Aragon, *Les Cloches de Bâle* (Paris: Denoël, 1934).

4. MARGUERITE DURAS

This discussion between Michel Foucault and Hélène Cixous was originally published in 1975: Michel Foucault, "A propos de Marguerite Duras," interview with Hélène Cixous, *Cahiers Renaud-Barrault* 89 (October 1975): 8–22. It was republished in *Dits et écrits*, ed. Daniel Defert, François Ewald, and Jacques Lagrange (Paris: Gallimard, 1994), 2:762–71.

1. Marguerite Duras, *Moderato cantabile*, trans. Richard Seaver (London: Calder and Boyars, 1966).

2. Marguerite Duras, *Destroy, She Said*, trans. Barbara Bray (New York: Grove, 1994); *Détruire dit-elle*, directed by Marguerite Duras, France, 1969.

5. PAUL'S STORY

This review by Michel Foucault of René Feret's *The Story of Paul* (1975) was originally published in 1975: Michel Foucault, "Faire les fous," *Le Monde*, no. 9559 (October 16, 1975): 17. It was republished in *Dits et écrits*, ed. Daniel Defert, François Ewald, and Jacques Lagrange (Paris: Gallimard, 1994), 2:802–5.

1. *Family Life*, directed by Ken Loach, United Kingdom, 1971.

6. THE NONDISCIPLINARY CAMERA VERSUS SADE

This interview conducted by Gérard Dupont in the French magazine *Cinématographe* was first published in 1975: Michel Foucault, "Sade, sergent du sexe," entretien avec Gérard Dupont, *Cinématographe*, no. 16 (December 1975–January 1976): 3–5. It was republished in *Dits et écrits*, ed. Daniel Defert, François Ewald, and Jacques Lagrange (Paris: Gallimard, 1994), 2:818–22.

1. *Translator's note*: This is a reference to Pier Paolo Pasolini's film *Salò, or the 120 Days of Sodom* (1975).

7. THE ASYLUM AND THE CARNIVAL

This discussion between Foucault and René Féret, director of *The Story of Paul* (1975), was originally published in 1976: Michel Foucault, "Sur 'Histoire de Paul,'" entretien avec René Féret, *Cahiers du cinéma*, no. 262–63 (January 1976): 63–65. It was republished in *Dits et eécrits*, ed. Daniel Defert, François Ewald, and Jacques Lagrange (Paris: Gallimard, 1994), 3:58–62.

8. CRIME AND DISCOURSE

This interview conducted by Pascal Kané, director of a short film titled *A propos de Pierre Rivière* (1976), about René Allio's film *Moi, Pierre Rivière, ayant égorgé ma mère, ma soeur et mon frère . . .* (1976), was originally published in 1976: Michel Foucault, "Entretien avec Michel Foucault, entretien avec Pascal Kané," *Cahiers du cinéma*, no. 271 (November 1976): 52–53. It was republished in *Dits et écrits*, ed. Daniel Defert, François Ewald, and Jacques Lagrange (Paris: Gallimard, 1994), 3:97–101.

1. Michel Foucault, ed., *I, Pierre Rivière, Having Slaughtered My Mother, My Sister, and My Brother: . . . A Case of Parricide in the 19th Century*, trans. Frank Jellinek (Lincoln: University of Nebraska Press, 1982).

9. THE RETURN OF PIERRE RIVIÈRE

This interview with Michel Foucault on René Allio's film *Moi, Pierre Rivière, ayant égorgé ma mère, ma soeur et mon frère* ... was originally published in 1976: Michel Foucault, "Le retour de Pierre Rivière," entretien avec G. Gauthier, *La revue du cinéma*, no. 312 (December 1976): 37–42. It was republished in *Dits et écrits*, ed. Daniel Defert, François Ewald, and Jacques Lagrange (Paris: Gallimard, 1994), 3:114–23.

1. Michel Foucault, ed., *I, Pierre Rivière, Having Slaughtered My Mother, My Sister, and My Brother* ... : *A Case of Parricide in the 19th Century*, trans. Frank Jellinek (Lincoln: University of Nebraska Press, 1982).
2. M. Antonioni, director, *Blow-Up*, 1966. Foucault and Antonioni had discussed their respective working methods.
3. Emmanuel Le Roy Ladurie, *Montaillou: The Promised Land of Error*, trans. Barbara Bray (New York: Braziller, 1978). Originally published in French in 1975.
4. *Le pain noir*, TV mini-series, created by Serge Moati, 1974–1975.

10. THE DULL REGIME OF TOLERANCE

This review of Pier Paolo Pasolini's film *Comizi d'amore* (*Love Meetings*) was originally published in 1977: Michel Foucault, "Les matins gris de la tolérance," *Le Monde*, no. 9998 (March 23, 1977): 24. It was republished in *Dits et écrits*, ed. Daniel Defert, François Ewald, and Jacques Lagrange (Paris: Gallimard, 1994), 3:269–71. The film was produced in Italy in 1963 and released in 1964.

1. Pier Paolo Pasolini, *Scritti corsari. Gli interventi più discussi di un testimone provocatorio*, Collana Memorie documenti (Milano: Garzanti, 1975); Pier Paolo Pasolini, *Écrits corsaires*, trans. Philippe Guilhon (Paris: Flammarion, 1976).

11. THE FOUR HORSEMEN OF THE APOCALYPSE

This interview was originally published in a special issue of *Cahiers du cinéma* in 1980: Michel Foucault, "Les quatres cavaliers de l'Apocalypse et les vermisseaux quotidiens," interview with B. Sobel, *Cahiers du cinéma*, no. 6, special issue: Syberberg (February 1980): 95–96. The introductory passage appears in Michel Foucault, "Les quatre cavaliers de l'Apocalypse et les vermisseaux quotidiens," in *Dits et écrits*, ed. Daniel Defert, François Ewald, and Jacques Lagrange (Paris: Gallimard, 1994), 4:102.

1. *Translator's note*: Simone Veil (1927–2017) was a prominent lawyer and politician who occupied senior positions in the French government and the European Parliament from 1956 to 1995. She was a survivor of the Auschwitz-Birkenau concentration camp.

12. WERNER SCHROETER AND MICHEL FOUCAULT IN CONVERSATION

This conversation was originally published in Michel Foucault, "Conversation avec Werner Schroeter, entretien avec et Gérard Courant et Werner Schroeter," December 3, 1981, in *Werner Schroeter*, ed. Gérard Courant (Paris: Goethe Institute, 1982), 39–47. It was republished in *Dits et écrits*, ed. Daniel Defert, François Ewald, and Jacques Lagrange (Paris: Gallimard, 1994), 4:251–60.

1. Foucault, "Conversation avec Werner Schroeter," 251. See "The Nondisciplinary Camera Versus Sade," chapter 6 in this volume.

2. *Translator's note*: Albert Camus wrote his play *Le malentendu* in 1943, and it was first performed in 1944. For an English translation with the title *Cross Purpose*, see Albert Camus, *Caligula & Other Plays: Caligula/ Cross Purpose/The Just/The Possessed*, trans. Stuart Gilbert, Justin O'Brien, and Henry Jones (Harmondsworth: Penguin in association with Hamish Hamilton, 1984).

3. *Translator's note*: Jean Eustache (1938–1981) was a post–New Wave French filmmaker, noted for his film *The Mother and the Whore* (1973).

4. Michel Foucault, *The Order of Things: An Archaeology of the Human Sciences* (London: Routledge, 2002), 422.

5. See Foucault's review of Chéreau's 1980 production: "The Imagination of the Nineteenth Century," in: *Essential Works of Foucault, 1954–1984*, vol. 2: *Aesthetics, Method, and Epistemology*, ed. James Faubion, trans. Robert Hurley (New York: New Press, 1998), 235–39.

APPENDIX

1. *Translator's note*: Only an extract of Patrice Maniglier and Dork Zabunyan's introduction to the program has been included here as the rest of the text appears in various forms in chapters 1 and 2 in this volume. The lists of films along with brief descriptions can be found at http://leclat.org/foucault_cinema1/; http://leclat.org/foucault_cinema2 /; and http://leclat.org/foucault_cinema3/. In the interests of brevity, I have added brief plot summaries in this appendix rather than translating the descriptions from the web pages. I have used the official English titles where they exist.

BIBLIOGRAPHY

WORKS BY MICHEL FOUCAULT

Michel Foucault. *The Archaeology of Knowledge and the Discourse on Language*. Translated by A. M. Sheridan Smith. New York: Pantheon, 1972.

——. *The Birth of the Clinic*. Translated by A. M. Sheridan. London: Tavistock, 1973.

——. "Anti-Rétro." Interview with Michel Foucault. *Cahiers du cinéma*, no. 251–52 (July–August 1974): 5–15. Republished in Michel Foucault, *Dits et écrits*, edited by Daniel Defert, François Ewald, and Jacques Lagrange, 2:646–60. Paris: Gallimard, 1994.

——. "A propos de Marguerite Duras." Interview with Hélène Cixous. *Cahiers Renaud-Barrault* 89 (October 1975): 8–22. Republished in Foucault, *Dits et écrits*, 2:762–71.

——. "Faire les fous." *Le Monde*, no. 9559 (October 16, 1975): 17. Republished in Foucault, *Dits et écrits*, 2:802–5.

——. "Sade, sergent du sexe." Interview with Gérard Dupont. *Cinématographe*, no. 16 (December 1975–January 1976): 3–5. Republished in Foucault, *Dits et écrits*, 2:818–22.

——. "Entretien avec Michel Foucault. Interview with Pascal Kané." *Cahiers du cinéma*, no. 271 (November 1976): 52–53. Republished in Foucault, *Dits et écrits*, 3:97–101.

——. "Le retour de Pierre Rivière." Interview with G. Gauthier. *La revue du cinéma*, no. 312 (December 1976): 37–42. Republished in Foucault, *Dits et écrits*, 3:114–23.

——. "Sur 'Histoire de Paul.' " Interview with René Féret. *Cahiers du cinéma*, no. 262–63 (January 1976): 63–65. Republished in Foucault, *Dits et écrits*, 3:58–62.

——. "Les matins gris de la tolérance." *Le Monde*, no. 9998, March 23, 1977, 24. Republished in Foucault, *Dits et écrits*, 3:269–71.

——. *The History of Sexuality*. Vol 1: *An Introduction*. Translated by Robert Hurley. New York, Pantheon, 1978.

——. "Les quatres cavaliers de l'Apocalypse et les vermisseaux quotidiens." Interview with Bernard Sobel. *Cahiers du cinéma*, no. 6, special issue: Syberberg (February 1980): 95–96. Republished in Foucault, *Dits et écrits*, 4:102–3.

——. "The Order of Discourse." In *Untying the Text: A Poststructuralist Reader*, edited by R. Young, translated by Ian McLeod, 48–78. Boston: Routledge and Kegan Paul, 1981.

——. "Conversation avec Werner Schroeter. Entretien avec et Gérard Courant et Werner Schroeter, December 3, 1981." In *Werner Schroeter*, edited by Gérard Courant, 39–47. Paris: Goethe Institute, 1982. Republished in Foucault, *Dits et écrits*, 4:251–60.

——, ed. *I, Pierre Rivière, Having Slaughtered My Mother, My Sister, and My Brother . . . : A Case of Parricide in the 19th Century*. Translated by Frank Jellinek. Lincoln: University of Nebraska Press, 1982.

——. "Preface." In *Anti-Oedipus, Capitalism and Schizophrenia*. By Gilles Deleuze and Félix Guattari. Translated by Robert Hurley, Mark Seem, and Helen R. Lane, xiii–xiv. Minneapolis: University of Minnesota Press, 1983.

——. *This Is Not a Pipe: With Illustrations and Letters by René Magritte*. Edited and translated by James Harkness. Berkeley: University of California Press, 1983.

——. "Nietzsche, Genealogy, History." In *The Foucault Reader*, edited by Paul Rabinow, 76–100. New York: Pantheon, 1984.

——. *The History of Sexuality*. Vol. 2: *The Use of Pleasure*. Translated by Robert Hurley. London: Penguin, 1985.

——. *Death and the Labyrinth: The World of Raymond Roussel*. Translated by Charles Ruas. London: Athlone, 1987.

——. "Power, Moral Values and the Intellectual." *History of the Present* 4 (1988): 1–13.

——. *The History of Sexuality*. Vol. 3: *The Care of the Self*. Translated by Robert Hurley. London: Penguin, 1990.

——. "Aller à Madrid." In Michel Foucault, *Dits et écrits*, 2:760–62.

——. *Dits et écrits*. 4 vols. Edited by Daniel Defert, François Ewald, and Jacques Lagrange. Paris: Gallimard, 1994.

——. *Discipline and Punish: The Birth of the Prison*. Translated by Alan Sheridan. New York: Vintage, 1995.

——. "The Concern for Truth." In *Foucault Live: Collected Interviews, 1961–1984*, edited by Sylvère Lotringer, translated by John Johnston, 455–64. New York: Semiotext(e), 1996.

——. "What Is Enlightenment?" In *Essential Works of Foucault, 1954–1984*. Vol. 1: *Ethics: Subjectivity and Truth*, edited by Paul Rabinow, translated by Catherine Porter, 303–19. New York: New Press, 1997.

——. "The Imagination of the Nineteenth Century." In *Essential Works of Foucault, 1954–1984*. Vol. 2: *Aesthetics, Method and Epistemology*, edited by James Faubion, translated by Robert Hurley, 235–39. New York: New Press, 1998.

——. "On the Ways of Writing History." In *Essential Works of Foucault, 1954–1984*, 2:279–95.

——. "Questions of Method." In *Essential Works of Foucault, 1954–1984*. Vol. 3: *Power*, edited by James D. Faubion, 223–38. New York: New Press, 2000.

——. *"Society Must Be Defended." Lectures at the Collège de France*. Edited by Mauro Bertani and Alessandro Fontana. Translated by David Macey. New York: Picador, 2001.

——. *The Order of Things: An Archaeology of the Human Sciences*. Translated by Alan Sheridan. London: Routledge Classics, 2002.

——. *La Peinture de Manet*. Edited by Maryvonne Saison. Paris: Éditions de Minuit, 2004.

——. *History of Madness*. Edited by Jean Khalfa. Translated by Jonathan Murphy and Jean Khalfa. London: Routledge, 2006.

——. *Psychiatric Power: Lectures at the Collège de France 1973–1974*. Edited by Jacques Lagrange. Translated by Graham Burchell. Basingstoke: Palgrave Macmillan, 2006.

——. *Manet and the Object of Painting*. Translated by Matthew Barr. London: Tate, 2011.

OTHER WORKS

Allio, René. *Carnets*. Paris: Lieu Commun, 1991.

Althusser, Louis. *For Marx*. Translated by Ben Brewster. London: Allen Lane, Penguin, 1969.

——. *Reply to John Lewis*. Translated by Grahame Locke. London: NLB, 1976.

Arendt, Hannah. *Eichmann in Jerusalem: A Report on the Banality of Evil*. New York: Viking, 1964.

Assayas, Olivier, Alain Bergala, Pascal Bonitzer, Serge Daney, Daniele Dubroux, Jean-Jacques Henry, Serge Le Péron, Jean Narboni, Guy-Parick Sainderichin, Louis Skorecki, Charles Tesson, and Serge Toubiana. "Dictionnaire sans foi ni loi." *Cahiers du cinéma*, no. 325 (June 1981): 116.

Baecque, Antoine de. *Les Cahiers du cinéma, histoire d'une revue*. Vol. 2: *Cinéma, tours et détours, 1959–1981*. Paris: Cahiers du cinéma. Diffusion, Seuil, 1991.

——. *L'histoire-camera*. Paris: Gallimard, 2008.

Balázs, Béla. *Béla Balázs: Early Film Theory. Visible Man and the Spirit of Film*. Edited by Erica Carter. Translated by Rodney Livingstone. New York: Berghahn, 2010.

Balibar, Étienne. "The Basic Concepts of Historical Materialism." In *Reading Capital: The Complete Edition*, by Louis Althusser, Etienne Balibar, Roger Establet, Pierre Macherey, and Jacques Rancière, translated by Ben Brewster and David Fernbach, 223–345. London: Verso, 2016.

——. *Violence and Civility. On the Limits of Political Philosophy*. Translated by G. M. Goshgarian. New York: Columbia University Press, 2016.

Bazin, André. "Will CinemaScope Save the Film Industry? (1953)." *Film-Philosophy* 6, no. 2 (January 2002). http://www.film-philosophy.com/index.php/f-p/article/view/666/579.

——. "William Wyler, or the Jansenist of Directing." In *Bazin at Work, Major Essays and Reviews from the Forties and Fifties*, edited by Bert Cardullo, translated by Alain Piette and Bert Cardullo, 1–22. London: Routledge, 1997.

Bloch, Marc. *French Rural History: An Essay on Its Basic Characteristics*. Translated by Janet Sondheimer. London: Routledge, 2015.

——. *The Historian's Craft.* Translated by Peter Putnam. Manchester: Manchester University Press, 1992.

Camus, Albert. *Caligula & Other Plays: Caligula/Cross Purpose/The Just/The Possessed.* Translated by Stuart Gilbert, Justin O'Brien, and Henry Jones. Harmondsworth: Penguin in association with Hamish Hamilton, 1984.

Cinémathèque française. "Programme: Foucault-Cinéma. Image mémoire, image pouvoir." October 22–31, 2004. http://lgm.meichler.free.fr/Nouveau %20dossier/foucault.pdf.

Collectif. *Intolérable. Textes réunis par le Groupe d'Information sur les Prisons.* Edited by Philippe Artières. Paris: Collection Verticales, Gallimard, 2013.

Daney, Serge. "Anti-Rétro (suite) et fonction critique (fin)." *Cahiers du cinéma,* no. 253 (October–November 1974): 20–36. Also published in Serge Daney, *La maison cinéma et le monde.* Vol. 1: *Le temps des* Cahiers *1962–1981,* edited by Patrice Rollet. Paris: POL, coll. Trafic, 2001.

——. "'Uranus' le deuil du deuil." In Serge Daney, *Devant la recrudescence des vols de sacs à main. Cinéma, télévision, information: 1988–1991.* Lyon: Aléas, 1991.

Deleuze, Gilles. *Cinema 1: The Movement-Image.* Translated by Hugh Tomlinson and Barbara Habberjam. Minneapolis: University of Minnesota Press, 1986.

——. *Cinema 2: The Time Image.* Translated by Hugh Tomlinson and Robert Galeta. Minneapolis: University of Minneapolis Press, 1989.

——. *Difference and Repetition.* Translated by Paul Patton. New York: Columbia University Press, 1994.

——. *Foucault.* Translated and edited by Séan Hand. London: Continuum, 1999.

——. "Foucault and Prisons." In *Two Regimes of Madness, Texts and Interviews 1975–1995,* edited by David Lapoujade, translated by Ames Hodges and Mike Taormina, 277–86. New York: Semiotext(e)/Foreign Agents, 2007.

——. *The Logic of Sense.* Edited by Constantin V. Boundas. Translated by Mark Lester and Charles Stivale. New York: Columbia University Press, 1993.

——. 'What Is a Dispositif?' In *Michel Foucault Philosopher,* edited by T. J. Armstrong, 159–68. Hemel Hempstead: Harvester Wheatsheaf, 1992.

——. "What Is the Creative Act?" In *Two Regimes of Madness, Texts and Interviews 1975–1995*, edited by David Lapoujade, translated by Ames Hodges and Mike Taormina. 317–29. New York: Semiotext(e)/Foreign Agents, 2007.

Duras, Marguerite. *Moderato cantabile*. Translated by Richard Seaver. Richmond: Oneworld Classics, 2008.

Eisenstein, Sergei. "A Dialectic Approach to Film Form." In *Film Form: Essays in Film Theory*, edited and translated by Jay Leda, 45–63. New York: Harcourt, 1977.

Epstein, Jean. *Écrits sur le cinéma, 1921–1953: édition chronologique en deux volumes*. Vol. 1: *1921–1947*. Edited by Pierre Lherminier. Paris: Cinéma Club/Seghers, 1975.

——. *Jean Epstein: Critical Essays and New Translations*. Edited by Sarah Keller and Jason N. Paul. Amsterdam: Amsterdam University Press, 2012.

Éribon, Didier. *Michel Foucault*. Translated by Betsy Wing. Cambridge, Mass.: Harvard University Press, 1991.

Farmer, Robert. "Jean Epstein." *Senses of Cinema* 57 (December 2010). http://sensesofcinema.com/2010/great-directors/jean-epstein/.

Gil, Marie. "Foucault invente l'histoire litteraire." *Fabula LHT (litterature, histoire, theorie)*, no. 0 (2005). http:// www.fabula.org/lht/o/Gil.html.

Gil, Marie, and Patrice Maniglier. "L'image-vengeance. Tarantino face à l'histoire. *Inglourious Basterds*." In *Quentin Tarantino: Un cinéma déchainé*, edited by Emmanuel Burdeau and Nicolas Vieillescazes, 100–121. Paris: Capricci/Les Prairies ordinaires, 2013.

Godard, Jean-Luc. Press conference at the Montreal Film Festival in, transcribed by Henri Béhar, *Film Scouts*. http://www.filmscouts.com/scripts/interview.cfm?ArticleCode=2800.

Greenberg, Clement. *Art and Culture. Critical Essays*. Boston: Beacon, 1961.

Lindeperg, Sylvie. *"Night and Fog": A Film in History*. Translated by Tom Mes. Minneapolis: University of Minnesota Press, 2014.

Maniglier, Patrice. "Anthropological Meditations: The Discourse on Comparative Method." In *Anthropology After Metaphysics*, edited by Pierre Charbonnier, Gildas Salmon, and Peter Skafish, 109–32. Lanham, Md.: Rowman & Littlefield, 2016.

——. "Foucault and *The Order of Things.*" In *A Companion to Michel Foucault*, edited by Christopher Falzon, Timothy O'Leary, and Jana Sawicki, 104–35. London: Wiley-Blackwell, 2013.

——. "Lanzmann philosophe (introduction au corps-Shoah)." In *Claude Lanzmann: Un voyant dans le siècle*, edited by Juliette Simont. Paris: Gallimard, 2017.

——. "Manifeste pour un comparatisme supérieur en philosophie." *Temps modernes*, no. 682 (July 2015): 86–145.

Mauss, Marcel. "The Techniques of the Body." Translated by Ben Brewster. *Economy and Society* 2, no. 1 (1973): 70–88.

Potte-Bonneville, Mathieu. *Michel Foucault, l'inquietude de l'histoire.* Paris: PUF, 2004.

Rancière, Jacques. *Film Fables.* Translated by Emiliano Battista. Oxford: Berg, 2006.

Raskin, Richard. *Nuit et Brouillard: On the Making, Reception and Functions of a Major Documentary Film.* Aarhus: Aarhus University Press, 1987.

Revel, Jacques. "Un exercise de désorientement: *Blow up.*" In *De l'histoire au cinéma*, edited by Antoine de Baecque and Christian Delage, 99–110. Paris: Complex, 2008.

Sartre, Jean-Paul. *Words.* Translated by Irene Clephane. London: Penguin Modern Classics, 2000.

Toubiana, Serge. "Michel Foucault et le cinéma." In *Michel Foucault, la littérature et les arts*, edited by Philippe Artières. Paris: Kimé, 2004.

Vertov, Dziga. *Kino-Eye: The Writings of Dziga Vertov.* Introduced and edited by Annette Michelson. Translated by Kevin O'Brien. Berkeley: University of California Press, 1984.

Veyne, Paul. "Foucault Revolutionizes History." In *Foucault and His Interlocutors*, edited by Arnold I. Davidson, 146–82. Chicago: University of Chicago Press, 1997.

Vinciguerra, Lucien. "Comment inverser exactement *Les Ménines*: Michel Foucault et la peinture à la fin des années 1960, des formes symboliques aux dispositifs." In *Le moment philosophique des années 1960 en France*, edited by Patrice Maniglier, 477–94. Paris: PUF, 2011.

Viveiros de Castro, Eduardo. *Cannibal Metaphysics.* Edited and translated by Peter Skafish. Minneapolis: Univocal, 2014.

Zabunyan, Dork. *Gilles Deleuze: Voir, parler, penser au risque du cinéma.* Paris: Presse Nouvelle Sorbonne, 2008.

——. "Un effet de blow up: philosophie, cinema et inconscient de l'histoire." In *Le moment philosophique des années soixante*, edited by Patrice Maniglier. Paris: PUF, 2011.

INDEX